Praise for
Dumbing Us Down

You've articulated in a most profound way the problems we are all observing in our students and children. My own 18-year-old commented that you clearly know what's going on.

— Cynthia Brown, Editor, *The International Educator*,
West Bridgwater MA

I'm still baffled by how someone so forthright would have been named Teacher of the Year.

— Jeanne Allen, Editor, *Education Update*,
Washington DC

... a masterful presentation of the "hidden curriculum." I can't think of anyone presently taking the public discussion of education so skillfully beyond where it usually gets stuck.

— Eugene J. Burkart, Attorney at Law,
Waltham MA

One of the world's most controversial education reformists.

— *The Western Australian*

...inspirational and chillingly on the money.

— Bruce Bebb, *The Hollywood Reporter*, Hollywood CA

You've got guts.

— D'Arcy Rickard, British Columbia School Trustees
Association, Canada

...everywhere we look these days your words are printed and reprinted and analyzed and criticized and applauded. Thanks for your common sense approach to it all.

— Mark and Helen Hegener, *Home Education Magazine*, Tonasket WA

Easily the most brilliant and arresting salvo on education that I've seen.

— Graham Betts, Madison WI

I read what you had to say with the greatest of delight and shared it with friends, one of whom said it brought tears to her eyes. We both thank you for writing.

— Edward M. Jones, Editor, *A Voice for Children*, Santa Fe NM

Your words hit the nail on the head. Our schools leave no time for kids to be with parents and the community.

— Bonni McKeown, Capon Springs VA

Professor Kenneth E. Boulding saw your writing and got it to me. I so fully agreed with everything you said that you have re-excited me about the similar mission I am on.

— Ed Lyell, Colorado State Board of Education, Denver CO

Everyone is listening to you. Thank goodness!

— Debbie Caldwell, Boston, MA

We found your views so resonant with the work we are doing that we reprinted excerpts from your speech. We have had many comments from our readers about the quality and truth of your words.

— Betsy Koenig, Executive Director, *The Renaissance Educator*, Loveland CO

Your book is excellent. You are an amazing writer, somehow able to be concise, sweeping and passionate all at the same time. Paulo Freire should have had to take one of your English classes. Unlike after reading Freire or Illich, I only wanted more when I got to the end of *Dumbing Us Down*.

— Chris Mercogliano, Director, The Albany Free School, Albany NY

A very important and passionate book — a reawakening of the penetrating critique of schooling made in the 1960s by John Holt, Jonathan Kozol, and James Herndon ... it deserves top be in every bookstore in the country. Yours is a voice of humanity, community and love. Bravo!

— Ron Miller, Editor, *Holistic Education Review*

My daughter, a smart, dedicated 14-year-old who just dropped out of high school and is successfully pursuing independent studies reports that your findings about the nature of institutional schooling are precisely right. Drove her nuts.

— Ken Richards, Richmond IN

I count this speech one of the best articles on education I ever read. I believe you have put your finger on the central problems and have illustrated what you are saying with wonderful data and personal experiences.

— Gene W. Marshall, Dallas TX

Brilliant. I've never seen so many true statements about education, children and families in one place. ...Your insights and integrity are wonderful.

— Norah Dooley, Cambridge MA

Seldom have I read such a penetrating and passionate diagnosis of our current educational and cultural crisis. And I have read all the current weighty expostulations.

— Robert Inchausti, California Polytechnic University, San Luis Obispo CA

I can visualize the Department of Education putting out a contract on your life. Please continue to speak out in the direction you are going.

— W. Evans, Woodbury/St.George UT

Your articles are wonderful and so desperately needed. I've copied them for a dozen families and everyone was enthusiastic. One mother said, "We should elect this man President!"

— Elaine Majors, Chapel Hill NC

Any student would be lucky to have a teacher like Gatto.

— Editorial in *Commonweal*

Thank you for challenging public education – in your *Wall Street Journal* editorial, your evening program at Carnegie Hall, your book, and all the rest.

— Sandra Booth, Spring Valley NY

It is as refreshing to read and hear your words as it is to study Zen… Good show!

— John Warfield, Huntingdon VA

Dumbing Us Down

The Hidden Curriculum of Compulsory Schooling

JOHN TAYLOR GATTO

Foreword by Thomas Moore

NEW SOCIETY PUBLISHERS

Cataloguing in Publication Data:

A catalog record for this publication is available from the National Library of Canada.

Copyright © 2005 by John Gatto.
All rights reserved. Original edition © 1992.

Cover design by Diane McIntosh from a painting by George Deem, *School of Balthus,* 1985 (detail). Oil on canvas. Courtesy Pavel Zoubok Gallery, New York. Photographed by Edward Peterson Jr.

Printed in Canada. Sixth printing February 2009.

Paperback ISBN: 978-0-86571-448-9

Inquiries regarding requests to reprint all or part of *Dumbing Us Down* should be addressed to New Society Publishers at the address below.

To order directly from the publishers, please call toll-free (North America) 1-800-567-6772, or order online at www.newsociety.com

Any other inquiries can be directed by mail to:

New Society Publishers

P.O. Box 189, Gabriola Island, BC V0R 1X0, Canada

250-247-9737

New Society Publishers' mission is to publish books that contribute in fundamental ways to building an ecologically sustainable and just society, and to do so with the least possible impact on the environment, in a manner that models this vision. We are committed to doing this not just through education, but through action. We are acting on our commitment to the world's remaining ancient forests by phasing out our paper supply from ancient forests worldwide. This book is one step towards ending global deforestation and climate change. It is printed on acid-free paper that is **100% old growth forest-free** (100% post-consumer recycled), processed chlorine free, and printed with vegetable based, low VOC inks. For further information, or to browse our full list of books and purchase securely, visit our website at: www.newsociety.com

NEW SOCIETY PUBLISHERS   www.newsociety.com

Dedication

I dedicate this book to my grandaughter,
Gudrun Moss Gunnarsdottir, whose name
in Icelandic means "the handwriting
of God," and to her mother, Briseis.
Sparkle and shine in the face of darkness,
you two light up the shadows.

Contents

Foreword

Thomas Moore

MY FATHER IS A BORN TEACHER. He's the kind of man who can spot a potential learner from a distance and go into action. When I was in my forties, he taught me how to bowl at his local bowling alley. In his typical fashion, he said, "Pick up the ball and roll it fast toward the center of those pins." That's all. He knew I could learn this relatively simple skill on my own. He believed in what John Gatto calls "self-teaching."

With my father's blood in me, I've been a teacher for forty years and have always loved the role. I learned it through apprenticeship with him. At eighty-eight, having retired from teaching plumbing in a trade school, he taught courses in a local school to adults who wanted to learn how to use computers. I hope I still have that kind of passion in my eighties.

But my father has also run up against the hardheaded bureaucracy John Gatto criticizes so explosively. Once, he approached a local school to tell them that, as a former plumbing instructor, he could give a talk to a class of children on where their drinking water comes from, how it's cleaned up, and where it goes after it's used. The school thanked him for the offer but told him there was no room on their schedule.

I thought the school missed the boat on many levels. My father knows how to talk to kids, and children need some practical learning. Who knows what rich rewards would have come to those children just from being in the presence of a real teacher who loved his material and loves children? And him teaching that class would also have been an act of community. John Gatto makes the important point that a community needs old people and children mixing together.

As a teacher I've done some things I consider relatively outrageous but nothing as profoundly educational as the efforts of John Gatto. Teaching piano, I've encouraged children to start by composing their own music, thumping the sides of the instrument for percussive effect if they are so inclined. I used to counsel a college student as she stood on the window well in my office, easing her shyness by remaining behind a curtain. A colleague once came in and saw a pair of shoes sticking out from the drapery and naturally wondered what was going on. The most enjoyable teaching I ever did took place in a classroom that had thick carpeting but no chairs. My thirty students had no textbooks, no syllabus, and no purpose. I picked up on whatever appeared in the room on any particular day and followed it through. I've never seen so much learning take place, for me and my students, anywhere else.

A physician once said to me that healing always takes place when her back is turned. For me, learning happens when the teacher has other things in mind. I believe this kind of learning can be shaped and even taught, not in schools as we know them, but, as John

Gatto says, when a mother and daughter take a trip to talk to a police chief or when some children learn how to put out a newsletter by apprenticing to a publisher. Learning can't take place in pieces of time cut out for the convenience of an institution or in lessons set apart from the world in which students live. We don't learn when life is divided up into sections that have little connection with each other.

I met John Gatto about ten years ago at a small gathering of educators. During the course of a day's activities, we were asked to present an object that meant something to us. I remember John grabbing an old briefcase that I think he said had belonged to his father. It had a beautiful patina and evidence everywhere of years of loving use. When I saw John lift that briefcase, my heart skipped. It was so much like my father to value such a thing and to feel the passing of a sensibility from father to son to grandson. A gesture like this reveals that a person is full of soul. My father could never teach English, as John Gatto does, but the two of them share a way of seeing things, a way that is precious beyond measure and always in danger of being lost.

What I love about John's writing is the lively combination of outrageous irreverence and an omnipresent cool intelligence: the ease with which he refers to school as a jail, as confinement, as a cell; school as a vampire network that should have a stake driven through its heart; school bells as inoculating each child with indifference. As a reader you have no doubt where John stands.

John's right — it won't do to tinker with schools and try to make them better. We have to start from the ground up and reconsider what education is. In my language, I'd like to see us educate the soul, and not just the mind. The result would be a person who could be in this world creatively, make good friendships, live in a place he loved, do work that is rewarding, and make a contribution to the community. People say that the word "educate" means to "draw out" a person's potential. But I like the "duc"-part in the middle of it. To be educated is to become a duke, a leader, a person of stature and color, a presence and a character.

I'm happy to see this passionate book coming to light once again. I celebrate it. I think it should be read aloud to educators and parents everywhere. I know it asks us to reconsider what we may think of as natural and obvious, but we need original ideas. Crumbling school buildings are telling us how tired they are. Violence in schools is screaming at us to stop doing this thing we call "teaching." The sorry level of discourse in America should tell us that the imaginations of our citizens are being cheated by the desperate ineffectiveness of schools. I'm grateful to John Gatto for having the gutsy imagination to tell us what's wrong and for giving us some good ideas on how to make it right.

October 2001

(Thomas Moore is the author of *Care of the Soul: A Guide for Cultivating Depth and Sacredness in Everyday Life, Soul Mates: Honoring the Mysteries of Love and Relationship*, and *The Re-Enchantment of Everyday Life*.)

Introduction

David Albert

AS ITS EDITOR AND FORMER PUBLISHER, I would have liked to flatter myself into believing that John Taylor Gatto's *Dumbing Us Down* was both his first book and his most popular. Unfortunately, and by a long stretch, neither is true. That will come as a surprise to many, who are most familiar with this book in its earlier green-and-black cover incarnation, or with John's two more recent books *The Underground History of American Education* (that's the big, fat one) and *A Different Kind of Teacher* (a blue hardcover).

John's first work was a set of Monarch Notes. Some of you may remember these from high school, a way to get by in English class without doing the required reading! At any rate, Gatto's first book was originally published in 1975, a Monarch Notes guide to Ken Kesey's *One Flew Over the Cuckoo's Nest*.

John related to me once — after affixing his signature on my copy, with handwriting only a hair more legible than my own (we must both have had Mr. Lewis in the 6th grade and still not recovered from the experience), and scribbling "Light up the darkness, keep the faith, and give the bastards the business!" into it — that the Monarch Notes guide, still in print after 26 years, has actually sold over two million copies, making it by far his most widely read work. But all he ever got out of it was a Burmese cat. If you ever get the opportunity to attend one of his talks, make sure to ask him about it.

Anyway, this Monarch Notes guide — the only book of Gatto's likely to be read by students undergoing their slow death in what passes for "educational institutions" these days — is an incendiary work. And not only because of its black-and-red cover.

Kesey's magnificent novel, as well as the excellent movie featuring a young Jack Nicholson (not recommended until you've read the book!), is the story of a rebel – one Randall Patrick McMurphy — who finds himself (or rather finds a way to get himself) inside a state psychiatric institution in the 1960s. Once within, he discovers himself bound by a web of rules, procedures, and protocols — really, kid gloves — behind which stands an iron fist of violence and repression, all designed of course for "the patient's own good." In scene after scene, McMurphy probes the boundaries of the forces that stand behind the institution — "the Combine" — which comes to be symbolized by "The Big Nurse" who controls the ward and ultimately holds the fate of each of the patients in her hands. Let me not ruin the book for you. I suggest you go out and read it, alongside your teenager if you have one, or, if you've read it once before, read it again, with new eyes.

Kesey's novel takes place against a backdrop of relentless institutional conditioning. While meetings on the ward may seem to be democratically organized and inmates — no, here they are called "patients" — are urged toward accountability, one quickly realizes that there is no democracy at work in the asylum and that accountability is a sham. Inmates are tracked, without their consent, into well-demarcated groups as acutes and chronics, and then further subdivided into walkers, wheelers, and vegetables. The highest value to the Combine is neither democracy nor accountability, but *compliance*, pure and simple, and its favorite strategem is to divide and conquer. And if that doesn't work, there are always drugs. Hmm.

I doubt that a set of Monarch Notes has ever been heaped with literary praise before, but Gatto's is much deserving. His description of the Keseyan institutional world contained in this incendiary set of crib notes (he even quotes Che Guevara: "Educate your enemy, don't kill him, for he is worth more to you alive than dead") is as compelling as the novel itself. He describes the Combine that controls this little world as "an all-powerful, earth-girdling, brain-destroying association of technocrats ... intent on building a world of precision, efficiency, and tidiness ... a place where the schedule is unbreakable." "In such a world," he writes, "there is neither grief nor happiness; nobody dies – they only burn out and are recycled; actually, it is a rather safe place, everything is planned – there are neither risks nor surprises." Gatto argues that within this world, "[w]ords and meaningless routines insulate people from life itself, blind them to what is happening around them, and deaden the moral faculties." The defense to this charge — ironic, of course, as he notes — is that the Big Nurse delivers charity baskets to the poor. Pivotal to Kesey's novel, according to Gatto, "is the cataclysmic revelation that the inmates of the asylum are not committed but are there of their own free will." And the way they are controlled, ultimately, is through guilt, shame, fear, and belittlement. Double hmmm.

And now, telescoping the next 25 years of his career, Gatto tells us the way out. "The way out of the asylum," he writes, "is literally to throw out the control panel, on a physical level smashing the reinforced windows, on a symbolic spiritual level becoming independent of rules, orders, and other people's urgencies." "Self-reliance," he concludes, "is the antidote to institutional stupidity."

We should all express our gratitude that John Gatto took his own advice and, beginning with *Dumbing Us Down*, has undertaken to tell us what life is really about "on the inside," as if, in our heart of hearts, we didn't already know. Like Chief Bromden — the supposedly deaf-and-dumb Indian in Kesey's novel who finally finds his own voice — he managed to steal away. Well, perhaps that's not the best possible description, for John has made rather a big splash! And I have been privileged to have helped the resultant wave along.

When I first read what was to become *Dumbing Us Down* in manuscript back in late 1989, it provided an almost unique answer to a conundrum I had not been able to figure out for myself. My older daughter was two at the time — long before my own book *And the Skylark Sings with Me* was even a glint in my eye. I was beginning to read up on education writers, both those who occupied the deep left end of the pond and those who swam in a "less sinister" direction.

What was most striking to me at the time — and remains so to this day — was how much they occupy the same pond. Their descriptions of the world of public education closely parallel each other, even if they view underlying causes differently. They all emphasize what seem to them to be the obvious deficiencies of public education. More often than not, though with different points of emphasis, they note the boredom, the mindless competition, the enforced social and economic stratification, the lack of any real engagement — academic or otherwise — the brutality and violence, the "soul-lessness" that characterizes what passes for education these days. From Alfie Kohn (liberal) to Thomas Sowell (conservative), they wax poetic about the shortcomings of modern schooling, though their antidotes are often worlds apart. And all my friends had stories of themselves as inmates (oh, sorry, I meant "students"), being shamed, embarrassed, harassed, brutalized, drugged, inflicted with boredom, or just plain ignored — and they remembered these experiences far more vividly than anything they were ever ostensibly taught.

And yet the idea that schools are failing didn't make any sense to me. After all, the schools are run by highly paid and educated public servants, hired by local elected school boards — my neighbors — staffed by people prepared in our graduate schools of education where they were, in turn, taught by faculty trained at our elite private universities such as Yale or the University of Chicago. Teachers are honored, school administrators with salaries well in excess of $100,000 receive merit raises, the school boards continue to get elected, the electorate continues to vote to give the schools more money, the graduate schools of education get bigger. If these are failing institutions, they sure have a funny way of showing it!

Gatto provided, and continues to provide the key to comprehending this conundrum. Central to this understanding is the fact that *schools are not failing.* On the contrary, they are spectacularly successful in doing precisely what they are intended to do, and what they have been intended to do since their inception. The system, perfected at places like the University of Chicago, Columbia Teachers College, Carnegie-Mellon, and Harvard, and funded by the captains of industry, was explicitly set up to ensure a docile, malleable workforce to meet the growing, changing demands of corporate capitalism — "to meet the new demands of the 20th century," they would have said back then. The Combine (whoops, slipped again!) ensures a workforce that will not rebel — the greatest fear at the turn of the 20th century — that will be physically, intellectually, and emotionally dependent upon corporate institutions for their incomes, self-esteem, and stimulation, and that will learn to find social meaning in their lives solely in the production and consumption of material goods. We all grew up in these institutions and we know they work. They haven't changed much since the 1890s because they don't need to – they perform precisely as they are intended.

In a recent lecture at which I introduced him, John cited U.S. Department of Labor statistics regarding the occupations most widely held by Americans today. The job that is held by the largest number of individuals, as well as the occupation that has shown the greatest growth in the past 30 years, is that of Wal-Mart clerk.* Second is McDonald's burger flipper. Third is Burger King flipper. And close behind? Elementary school teacher. The main difference between these jobs and those held in the days of Henry Ford in the early part of the 20th century is that Henry Ford wanted to be able to pay his workers enough so that they would be able to afford new automobiles (and food and houses and medical care) themselves and thus provide the consumption engine guaranteeing the profitability of the corporation. Now, with globalization of the marketplace, it is undeniably clear that the captains of industry no longer care.

What do they really care about? That public education be public. In other words, that we — and not they — pay for it. Corporate institutions have unloaded their basic training needs on to us, and we voluntarily pay to forge the chains of our own servitude.

So far, so good. But the obvious question that follows from this is this: If educational institutions are so demonstrably successful, why are we always hearing about their failures? And here Gatto might have provided the answer, for in his aborted career before becoming a New York City schoolteacher, one decade before Monarch Notes and almost four before this edition of *Dumbing Us Down*, he was an advertising copywriter, "a young fellow," as he writes in The Green Monongahela, "with a knack for writing thirty-second television commercials." The copywriter knows that to sell a product or

---

*In fact the number of people employed by Wal-Mart and their families is greater than the population of each of the following states: Alabama, Alaska, Arkansas, Colorado, Connecticut, Delaware, Hawaii, Idaho, Iowa, Kansas, Kentucky, Louisiana, Maine, Mississippi, Montana, Nebraska, Nevada, New Hampshre, New Mexico, North Dakota, Oklahoma, Oregon, Rhode Island, South Carolina, South Dakota, Utah, Vermont, West Virginia, and Wyoming.

service, one must create the perception of need and the palpable feeling that this need can only be filled exclusively through the purchase of the product or service being sold. The simplistic notion that "our schools are failing" easily translates into a limitless demand for more resources for the institution and its supports: for books, for teachers, for computers, for real estate (and hence for book publishers, graduate schools of education, computer manufacturers, and real estate developers) — and for more time: for more pre-school, more homework, longer school years, the end of recess, and semi- (and soon fully) compulsory summer schools. And to the copywriter's delight, it's a zero-sum game. Not only is there an endless stream of consumers with little or no institutional memory and an absolutely insatiable demand, but the truth is that no matter how much is expended in the educational marketplace, 50% of the schools will remain "below average", with those branded as poor performers changing from year to year and those above the mid-point fearing, above all, that they will fall into the abyss. And the copywriter has done his job for, it is universally believed, the only response to a fall into sub-mediocrity is to buy one's way out.

This stratagem is extraordinarily elegant but so transparent that it always ran the risk of being seen for the confidence game that, at bottom, it is, except that it gets translated down to individual children. In other words, the Combine preys upon our maternal and paternal instincts. And so the latest iteration of "education reform" (the fifth such set of reforms in my brief lifespan) comes with new (actually old) testing strategies where it can be ensured that large majorities of children will regularly "fail", either in comparison with each other, with those in another school, or with children living in the much more productive economies of Tunisia or Slovenia. The "answer" to those deficits and the perpetual dissatisfaction they engender is simply more of the same, rather like "the hair of the dog that bit you".

The reforms are therefore never completed. To do so would require admitting failure, or worse, admitting that the failure is not failure at all, only a continuing round in the socialized enforcement of intellectual and emotional dependency, of which Gatto writes so eloquently. In the meantime, what we're doing is like requiring our children to live in buildings that are never finished, and never will be, and forcing them to breathe in the noxious fumes and dirt and dust from the never-ending construction.

But our children deserve the opportunity to come up for a breath of fresh air.

❖　❖　❖

Fresh air, however, is going to be difficult to find.

Dan Greenberg, founder of the Sudbury Valley School — a successful 30-year-old learning community based on the principles of self-initiated learning and democratic self-government — has written that between leading educators, business leaders, and government officials there is a virtually unanimous agreement regarding the essential features of an education that would meet the needs of society in the 21st century. He sees consensus on six points:

- As society rapidly changes, individuals will have to be able to function comfortably in a world that is always in flux. Knowledge will continue to increase at a dizzying rate. This means that a content-based curriculum, with a set body of information to be imparted to students, is entirely inappropriate as a means of preparing children for their adult roles.
- People will be faced with greater individual responsibility to direct their own lives. Children must grow up in an environment that stresses self-motivation and self -assessment. Schools that focus on external motivating factors, such as rewards and punishments for meeting goals set by others, are denying children the tools they need most to survive.
- The ability to communicate with others, to share experiences, to collaborate, and to exchange information is critical. Conversation, the ultimate means of communication, must be a central part of a sound education.
- As the world moves toward universal recognition of individual rights within a democratic society, people must be empowered to participate as equal partners in whatever enterprise they are engaged in. Students (and teachers) require full participation in running educational institutions, including the right to radically change them when needed.
- Technology now makes it possible for individuals to learn whatever they wish, whenever they wish, and in the manner they wish. Students should be empowered with both the technology and the responsibility for their own learning and educational timetable.

- Children have an immense capacity for concentration and hard work when they are passionate about what they are doing, and the skills they acquire in any area of interest are readily transferable to other fields. Schools must thus become far more tolerant of individual variation and far more reliant on self-initiated activities.

Gatto shares Greenberg's vision of what education should be like (and is supportive of all ventures that would bring it to fruition, even for just a few), but having spent the better part of three decades in the trenches, he has a far more realistic, if darker, view of the purposes to which education is put. He views school, as he writes in *The Underground History of American Education*, "as a conflict pitting the needs of social machinery against those of the human spirit, a war of mechanisms against flesh and blood that only require a human architect to get launched."

Let's put it plainly: in Gatto's view, the Combine needs dumb adults, and so it ensures the supply by making the kids dumb. From this perspective it is clear that Dan Greenberg is wrong. While there is always a need for a highly circumscribed number of technocrats to replace themselves, the Combine has only limited use for hundreds of millions of self-reliant, critically thinking individuals who engage in conversation and who determine their own needs as individuals and communities free of the Combine's enticements and commands. In fact, when such individuals exist, the Combine fears them. It may occasionally pay lip-service to their value, but it ultimately has no real use for artists, dancers, poets, self-sufficient farmers, tree lovers, devoted followers of what it views as non-materialist cults — Christian or otherwise — handicraft workers, makers of their own beer, or, for that matter, stay-at-home moms and dads, all of whom, when they endure at all, do so at the margins and on the periphery of the social economy. What the Combine needs, most of all, is Wal-Mart clerks and burger flippers and dedicated but low-paid, government-employed "foreign service officers" proud of their titles as teachers, who prevent the restless natives from rebelling while the extraction of resources and capital, human and otherwise, continues unabated. And, in the final analysis, while it employs the most extraordinary of spin-doctors and apologists, the Combine makes no compromises and takes no prisoners, not until it has colonized every nerve ending — every minute part and every habit of mind — as much as it has passed over every square inch of this good earth.

But the strategy doesn't work entirely. For every McMurphy who has had his brain fried, there is the possibility of a Chief Bromden who escapes. There are weeds growing in the cracks in the highway that will not be stamped out. We — the weeds — are here: you and I and Dan Greenberg and the author of our incendiary book. There are now a million homeschoolers, and there will soon be another million homeschool alumni. And with us, maybe, just maybe, and unlike what happened with any of the abortive alternative school movements of the past century, will come the power — with enough weeds grown up into tall trees — to block the highway as the Combine with engines blazing moves down our path.

Gatto implies through his writing, his life, and his witness that he does not believe individual solutions are likely to be the answer to larger societal problems — they may not by themselves destroy the Combine. But he has also demonstrated — and this Tenth Anniversary Edition of *Dumbing Us Down* celebrates this insight — that we can only stand to gain by protecting and enlarging those meager zones of freedom we inhabit, that is by widening the cracks in the pavement and by beginning to recapture that common energy, creativity, and imagination with which we are endowed by Great Nature as children, and which holds out the promise of better times to come.

Olympia, Washington
September 5, 2001

(David Albert is the author of *And the Skylark Sings With Me: Adventures in Homeschooling and Community-Based Education*, New Society Publishers, 1999.)

Publisher's Note

from the First Edition

THE SOCIAL PHILOSOPHER Hannah Arendt once wrote that, "The aim of totalitarian education has never been to instill conviction but to destroy the capacity to form any."*

If one were to poll our nation's leading educators about what the goal of our educational systems should be, I suspect one would come up with as many goals as educators. But I also imagine that the capacity to form one's own convictions independent of what was being taught in the classroom, the ability to think critically based upon one's own experience, would not rank high on many lists. In fact, the idea that the goal of education might have little to do with what goes on in the classroom would likely strike most educators, of whatever political stripe, as heresy.

In the context of our culture, it is easy to see that critical thinking is a threat. As parents, we all want what is "best" for our children. Yet, by our own actions and lifestyles, and through the demands that we place on our educational institutions, it is clear that by "best" we all too often mean "most." This shift from the qualitative to the quantitative, from thinking about what is best or the holistic development of the individual human being

*Hannah Arendt, *Totalitarianism* (New York: Harcourt Brace Jovanovich, 1968), p. 168.

to thinking about what resources should be available to semi-monopoly governmental educational institutions certainly does not bear close scrutiny.

Shouldn't we also ask ourselves what the consequences are of scrambling to provide the "most"" of everything to our children in a world of fast-dwindling resources? What does the mad and often brutally competitive scramble for resources – for more pay for teachers, for more equipment, for more money for schools – teach our children about us? More crucially, what message does this mad scramble send to those children who, through no fault of their own, lose out in the competition? And what would be the cost to the social fabric if our children's convictions were based on their experience? (Perhaps we are already paying the cost of the development of such convictions, however poorly articulated, in the forms of violence, chemical dependency, teenage pregnancy, and a host of other social ills affecting today's young people?)

Eclectic, engaging, and not readily pigeon-holed, John Taylor Gatto's thinking forces us to re-examine some of our most cherished assumptions in the light of his and his students' day-to-day experience. He provides few ready-made solutions or optimistic answers for the future of our schools. What he does provide through the example of his thirty years of teaching is, first, a commitment to providing *quality* options to the poor and disadvantaged, who are most in need of them, and, second, conscientization so that at least his students come to some critical understanding of what is being done to them in the name of "schooling."

Gatto's vision of our social order may be bleak, but it also provides at least a ray of hope in the example and idea that free-thinking and critically aware individuals, freely united in newly reconstructed communities, can correct social ills and lead us toward a future truly worth living in. Because we share the conviction that this is both desirable and possible, we at New Society Publishers are proud to publish *Dumbing Us Down*.

David H. Albert
for New Society Publishers
June 13, 1991

About the Author

I'M HERE TO TALK TO YOU ABOUT IDEAS, but I think a purpose might be served in telling a little bit about myself so I become a person like you rather than just another talking head from the television set. I know that sometimes when I hear a news report from TV I wonder, Who are *you*? and, Why are you telling me these things? So let me offer you some of the ground out of which these ideas grew.

I've worked as a New York City schoolteacher for the past thirty years, teaching for some of that time elite children from Manhattan's Upper West Side between Lincoln Center, where the opera is, and Columbia University, where the defense contracts are; and teaching, in most recent years, children from Harlem and Spanish Harlem whose lives are shaped by the dangerous undercurrents of the industrial city in decay. I've taught at six different schools in that time. My present school is in the shadow of St. John the Divine Cathedral, the largest Gothic structure in the United States, and not a long walk from the famous Museum of Natural History and the Metropolitan Museum of Art. About three blocks from my school is the spot where the "Central Park jogger" (as media mythology refers to her) was raped and brutally beaten a few years ago — seven of the nine attackers went to school in my district.

My own perspective on things, however, was shaped a long way from New York City, in the river town of Monongahela, Pennsylvania, forty miles southeast of Pittsburgh. In those days, Monongahela was a place of steel mills and coal mines, of paddle-wheel river steamers churning the emerald green water chemical orange, of respect for hard work and family life. Monongahela was a place with muted class distinctions since everyone was more or less poor, although very few, I suspect, knew they were poor. It was a place where independence, toughness, and self-reliance were honored, a place where pride in ethnic and local culture was very intense. It was an altogether wonderful place to grow up, even to grow up poor. People talked to each other, minding each other's business instead of the abstract business of "the world." Indeed, the larger world hardly extended beyond Pittsburgh, a wonderful dark steel city worth a trip to see once or twice a year. Nobody in my memory felt confined by Monongahela or dwelled, within my earshot, on the possibility they were missing something important by not being elsewhere.

My grandfather was the town printer and had been for a time the publisher of the town newspaper, *The Daily Republican* — a name that attracted some attention because the town was a stronghold of the Democratic Party. From my grandfather and his independent German ways I learned a great deal that I might have missed if I had grown up in a time, like today, when old people are put away in a home or kept out of sight.

Living in Manhattan has been for me in many ways like living on the moon. Even though I've been here for thirty-five years, my heart and habit are still in Monongahela. Nevertheless, the shock of Manhattan's very different society and values sharpened my sense of difference and made me an anthropologist as well as a schoolteacher. Over the past thirty years, I've used my classes as a laboratory where I could learn a broader range of what human possibility is — the whole catalogue of hopes and fears — and also as a place where I could study what releases and what inhibits human power.

During that time, I've come to believe that genius is an exceedingly common human quality, probably natural to most of us. I didn't want to accept that notion — far from it: my own training in two elite universities taught me that intelligence and talent distributed themselves economically over a bell curve and that human destiny, because of those mathematical, seemingly irrefutable scientific facts, was as rigorously determined as John Calvin contended.

The trouble was that the unlikeliest kids kept demonstrating to me at random moments so many of the hallmarks of human excellence — insight, wisdom, justice, resourcefulness, courage, originality — that I became confused. They didn't do this often enough to make my teaching easy, but they did it often enough that I began to wonder, reluctantly, whether it was possible that being in school itself was what was dumbing them down. Was it possible I had been hired not to enlarge children's power, but to diminish it? That seemed crazy on the face of it, but slowly I began to realize that the bells and the confinement, the crazy sequences, the age-segregation, the lack of privacy, the constant surveillance, and all the rest of the national curriculum of schooling were designed exactly as if someone had set out to *prevent* children from learning how to think and act, to coax them into addiction and dependent behavior.

Bit by bit I began to devise guerrilla exercises to allow as many of the kids I taught as possible the raw material people have always used to educate themselves: privacy, choice, freedom from surveillance, and as broad a range of situations and human associations as my limited power and resources could manage. In simpler terms, I tried to maneuver them into positions where they would have a chance to be their own teachers and to make themselves the major text of their own education.

In theoretical, metaphorical terms, the idea I began to explore was this one: that teaching is nothing like the art of painting, where, by the *addition* of material to a surface, an image is synthetically produced, but more like the art of sculpture, where, by the *subtraction* of material, an image already locked in the stone is enabled to emerge. It is a crucial distinction.

In other words, I dropped the idea that I was an expert whose job it was to fill the little heads with my expertise, and began to explore how I could remove those obstacles that prevented the inherent genius of children from gathering itself. I no longer felt comfortable defining my work as bestowing wisdom on a struggling classroom audience. Although I continue to this day in those futile assays because of the nature of institutional teaching, wherever possible I have broken with teaching tradition and sent kids down their separate paths to their own private truths.

The sociology of government monopoly schools has evolved in such a way that a premise like mine jeopardizes the total institution if it spreads. Kept contained, the occasional teacher who makes a discovery like mine is at worst an annoyance to the chain of command (which has evolved automatic defenses to isolate such bacilli and then to neutralize or destroy them). But once loose, the idea could imperil the central assumptions which allow the institutional school to sustain itself, such as the false assumption that it is difficult to learn to read, or that kids resist learning, and many more. Indeed, the very stability of our economy is threatened by any form of education that might change the nature of the human product schools now turn out: the economy school-children currently expect to live under and serve would not survive a generation of young people trained, for example, to think critically.

Success in my practice involves a large component of automatic trust, categorical trust, not the kind conditional on performance. People have to be allowed to make their own mistakes and to try again, or they will never *master* themselves, although they may well *seem* to be competent when they have in fact only memorized or imitated someone else's performance. Success in my practice also involves challenging many comfortable assumptions about what is worth learning and out of what material a good life is fashioned.

Over the years of wrestling with the obstacles that stand between child and education I have come to believe that government monopoly schools are structurally unreformable. They cannot function if their central myths are exposed and abandoned. Over the years I have come to see that whatever I thought I was doing as a teacher, most of what I actually was doing was teaching an invisible curriculum that reinforced the myths of the school institution and those of an economy based on caste. When I was trying to decide what to say to you that might make my experience as a schoolteacher useful, it occurred to me that I could best serve by telling you what I do that is wrong, rather than what I do that is right. What I do that is right is simple to understand: I get out of kids' way, I give them space and time and respect. What I do that is wrong, however, is strange, complex, and frightening. Let me begin to show you what that is.

Chapter

1

THE SEVEN-LESSON
SCHOOLTEACHER

*This speech was given on the occasion of the author being named
"New York State Teacher of the Year" for 1991.*

II

CALL ME MR. GATTO, PLEASE. Thirty years ago, having nothing better to do with myself at the time, I tried my hand at schoolteaching. The license I have certifies that I am an instructor of English language and English literature, but that isn't what I do at all. I don't teach English; I teach school — and I win awards doing it.

Teaching means different things in different places, but seven lessons are universally taught from Harlem to Hollywood Hills. They constitute a national curriculum you pay for in more ways than you can imagine, so you might as well know what it is. You are at liberty, of course, to regard these lessons any way you like, but believe me when I say I intend no irony in this presentation. These are the things I teach; these are the things you pay me to teach. Make of them what you will.

1. Confusion

A lady named Kathy wrote this to me from Dubois, Indiana, the other day:

> What big ideas are important to little kids? Well, the biggest idea I think they need is that what they are learning isn't idiosyncratic — that there is some system to it all and it's not just raining down on them as they helplessly absorb. That's the task, to understand, to make coherent.

Kathy has it wrong. *The first lesson I teach is confusion. Everything* I teach is out of context. I teach the un-relating of everything. I teach disconnections. I teach too much: the orbiting of planets, the law of large numbers, slavery, adjectives, architectural drawing, dance, gymnasium, choral singing, assemblies, surprise guests, fire drills, computer languages, parents' nights, staff-development days, pull-out programs, guidance with strangers my students may never see again, standardized tests, age-segregation unlike anything seen in the outside world ... What do any of these things have to do with each other?

Even in the best schools a close examination of curriculum and its sequences turns up a lack of coherence, a host of internal contradictions. Fortunately the children have no words to define the panic and anger they feel at *constant violations of natural order and sequence* fobbed off on them as quality in education. The logic of the school-mind is that it is better to leave school with a tool kit of superficial jargon derived from economics, sociology, natural science, and so on than with one genuine enthusiasm. But quality in education entails learning about something in depth. Confusion is thrust upon kids by too many strange adults, each working alone with only the thinnest relationship with each other, pretending, for the most part, to an expertise they do not possess.

Meaning, not disconnected facts, is what sane human beings seek, and education is a set of codes for processing raw data into meaning. Behind the patchwork quilt of school sequences and the school obsession with facts and theories, the age-old human search for meaning lies well concealed. This is harder to see in elementary school where the hierarchy of school experience seems to make better sense because the good-natured simple relationship between "let's do this" and "let's do that" is just assumed to mean something and the clientele has not yet consciously discerned how little substance is behind the play and pretense.

Think of the great natural sequences — like learning to walk and learning to talk; the progression of light from sunrise to sunset; the ancient procedures of a farmer, a smithy, or a shoemaker; or the preparation of a Thanksgiving feast. All of the parts are in perfect harmony with each other, each action justifying itself and illuminating the past and the future. School sequences aren't like that, not inside a single class and not among the total menu of daily classes. School sequences are crazy. There is no particular reason for any of them, nothing that bears close scrutiny. Few teachers would dare to teach the tools whereby dogmas of a school or a teacher could be criticized, since everything must be accepted. School subjects are learned, if they *can* be learned, like children learn the catechism or memorize the Thirty-nine Articles of Anglicanism.

I teach the un-relating of everything, an infinite fragmentation the opposite of cohesion; what I do is more related to television programming than to making a scheme of order. In a world where home is only a ghost because both parents work, or because of too many moves or too many job changes or too much ambition, or because something else has left everybody too confused to maintain a family relation, I teach students how to accept confusion as their destiny. That's the first lesson I teach.

2. CLASS POSITION

The second lesson I teach is class position. I teach that students must stay in the class where they belong. I don't know who decides my kids belong there but that's not my business. The children are numbered so that if any get away they can be returned to the right class. Over the years the variety of ways children are numbered by schools has increased dramatically, until it is hard to see the human beings plainly under the weight of numbers they carry. Numbering children is a big and very profitable undertaking, though what the strategy is designed to accomplish is elusive. I don't even know why parents would, without a fight, allow it to be done to their kids.

In any case, that's not my business. My job is to make them like being locked together with children who bear numbers like their own. Or at least to endure it like good sports. If I do my job well, the kids can't even *imagine* themselves somewhere else because I've shown them how to envy and fear the better classes and how to have contempt for the dumb classes. Under this efficient discipline the class mostly polices itself into good marching order. That's the real lesson of any rigged competition like school. You come to know your place.

In spite of the overall class blueprint that assumes that ninety-nine percent of the kids are in their class to stay, I nevertheless make a public effort to exhort children to higher levels of test success, hinting at eventual transfer from the lower class as a reward. I frequently insinuate the day will come when an employer will hire them on the basis of test scores and grades, even though my own experience is that employers are rightly indifferent to such things. I never lie outright, but I've come to see that truth and schoolteaching are, at bottom, incompatible, just as Socrates said thousands of years ago. The lesson of numbered classes is that everyone has a proper place in the pyramid and that there is no way out of your class except by number magic. Failing that, you must stay where you are put.

3. INDIFFERENCE

The third lesson I teach is indifference. I teach children not to care too much about anything, even though they want to make it appear that they do. How I do this is very subtle. I do it by demanding that they become totally involved in my lessons, jumping up and down in their seats with anticipation, competing vigorously with each other for my favor. It's heartwarming when they do that; it impresses everyone, even me. When I'm at my best I plan lessons very carefully in order to produce this show of enthusiasm. But when the bell rings I insist they drop whatever it is we have been doing and proceed quickly to the next work station. They must turn on and off like a light switch. Nothing important is ever finished in my class nor in any class I know of. Students never have a complete experience except on the installment plan.

Indeed, the lesson of bells is that no work is worth finishing, so why care too deeply about anything? Years of bells will condition all but the strongest to a world that can no longer offer important work to do. Bells are the secret logic of school time; their logic is inexorable. Bells destroy the past and future, rendering every interval the same as any other, as the abstraction of a map renders every living mountain and river the same, even though they are not. Bells inoculate each undertaking with indifference.

4. EMOTIONAL DEPENDENCY

The fourth lesson I teach is emotional dependency. By stars and red checks, smiles and frowns, prizes, honors, and disgraces, I teach kids to surrender their will to the predestinated chain of command. Rights may be granted or withheld by any authority without appeal, because rights do not exist inside a school — not even the right of free speech, as the Supreme Court has ruled — unless school authorities say they do. As a schoolteacher, I intervene in many personal decisions, issuing a pass for those I deem legitimate and initiating a disciplinary confrontation for behavior that threatens my control. Individuality is constantly trying to assert itself among children and teenagers, so my judgments come thick and fast. Individuality is a contradiction of class theory, a curse to all systems of classification.

Here are some common ways in which individuality shows up: children sneak away for a private moment in the toilet on the pretext of moving their bowels, or they steal a private instant in the hallway on the grounds they need water. I know they don't, but I allow them to "deceive" me because this conditions them to depend on my favors. Sometimes free will appears right in front of me in pockets of children angry, depressed, or happy about things outside my ken; rights in such matters cannot be recognized by schoolteachers, only privileges that can be withdrawn, hostages to good behavior.

5. INTELLECTUAL DEPENDENCY

The fifth lesson I teach is intellectual dependency. Good students wait for a teacher to tell them what to do. This is the most important lesson of them all: we must wait for other people, better trained than ourselves, to make the meanings of our lives. The expert makes all the important choices; only I, the teacher, can determine what my kids must study, or rather, only the people who pay me can make those decisions, which I then enforce. If I'm told that evolution is a fact instead of a theory, I transmit that as ordered, punishing deviants who resist what I have been told to tell them to think. This power to control what children will think lets me separate successful students from failures very easily.

Successful children do the thinking I assign them with a minimum of resistance and a decent show of enthusiasm. Of the millions of things of value to study, I decide what few we have time for. Actually, though, this is decided by my faceless employers. The choices are theirs — why should I argue? Curiosity has no important place in my work, only conformity.

Bad kids fight this, of course, even though they lack the concepts to know what they are fighting, struggling to make decisions for themselves about what they will learn and when they will learn it. How can we allow that and survive as schoolteachers? Fortunately there are tested procedures to break the will of those who resist; it is more difficult, naturally, if the kids have respectable parents who come to their aid, but that happens less and less in spite of the bad reputation of schools. No middle-class parents I have ever met actually believe that *their* kid's school is one of the bad ones. Not one single parent in many years of teaching. That's amazing, and probably the best testimony to what happens to families when mother and father have been well-schooled themselves, learning the seven lessons.

Good people wait for an expert to tell them what to do. It is hardly an exaggeration to say that our entire economy depends upon this lesson being learned. Think of what might fall apart if children weren't trained to be dependent: the social services could hardly survive — they would vanish, I think, into the recent historical limbo out of which they arose. Counselors and therapists would look on in horror as the supply of psychic invalids vanished. Commercial entertainment of all sorts, including television, would wither as people learned again how to make their own fun. Restaurants, the prepared food industry, and a whole host of other assorted food services would be drastically down-sized if people returned to making their own meals rather than depending on strangers to plant, pick, chop, and cook for them. Much of modern law, medicine, and engineering would go too, as well as the clothing business and schoolteaching, unless a guaranteed supply of helpless people continued to pour out of our schools each year.

Don't be too quick to vote for radical school reform if you want to continue getting a paycheck. We've built a way of life that depends on people doing what they are told because they don't know how to tell *themselves* what to do. It's one of the biggest lessons I teach.

6. PROVISIONAL SELF-ESTEEM

The sixth lesson I teach is provisional self-esteem. If you've ever tried to wrestle into line kids whose parents have convinced them to believe they'll be loved in spite of anything, you know how impossible it is to make self-confident spirits conform. Our world wouldn't survive a flood of confident people very long, so I teach that a kid's self-respect should depend on expert opinion. My kids are constantly evaluated and judged.

A monthly report, impressive in its provision, is sent into a student's home to elicit approval or mark exactly, down to a single percentage point, how dissatisfied with the child a parent should be. The ecology of "good" schooling depends on perpetuating dissatisfaction, just as the commercial economy depends on the same fertilizer. Although some people might be surprised how little time or reflection goes into making up these mathematical records, the cumulative weight of these objective-seeming documents establishes a profile that compels children to arrive at certain decisions about themselves and their futures based on the casual judgment of strangers. Self-evaluation, the staple of every major philosophical system that ever appeared on the planet, is never considered a factor. The lesson of report cards, grades, and tests is that children should not trust themselves or their parents but should instead rely on the evaluation of certified officials. People need to be told what they are worth.

7. ONE CAN'T HIDE

The seventh lesson I teach is that one can't hide. I teach students that they are always watched, that each is under constant surveillance by me and my colleagues. There are no private spaces for children; there is no private time. Class change lasts exactly three hundred seconds to keep promiscuous fraternization at low levels. Students are encouraged to tattle on each other or even to tattle on their own parents. Of course, I encourage parents to file reports about their own child's waywardness too. A family trained to snitch on itself isn't likely to conceal any dangerous secrets.

I assign a type of extended schooling called "homework," so that the effect of surveillance, if not the surveillance itself, travels into private households, where students might otherwise use free time to learn something unauthorized from a father or mother, by exploration or by apprenticing to some wise person in the neighborhood. Disloyalty to the idea of schooling is a devil always ready to find work for idle hands.

The meaning of constant surveillance and denial of privacy is that no one can be trusted, that privacy is not legitimate. Surveillance is an ancient imperative, espoused by certain influential thinkers, a central prescription set down in *The Republic, The City of God, The Institutes of the Christian Religion, New Atlantis, Leviathan,* and a host of other places. All the childless men who wrote these books discovered the same thing: children must be closely watched if you want to keep a society under tight central control. Children will follow a private drummer if you can't get them into a uniformed marching band.

II

It is the great triumph of compulsory government monopoly mass schooling that among even the best of my fellow teachers, and among even the best of my students' parents, only a small number can imagine a different way to do things. "The kids have to know how to read and write, don't they?" "They have to know how to add and subtract, don't they?" "They have to learn to follow orders if they ever expect to keep a job."

Only a few lifetimes ago things were very different in the United States. Originality and variety were common currency; our freedom from regimentation made us the miracle of the world; social-class boundaries were relatively easy to cross; our citizenry was marvelously confident, inventive, and able to do much for themselves independently, and to think for themselves. We were something special, we Americans, all by ourselves, without government sticking its nose into and measuring every aspect of our lives, without institutions and social agencies telling us how to think and feel. We were something special, as individuals, as Americans.

But we've had a society essentially under central control in the United States since just after the Civil War, and such a society requires compulsory schooling — government monopoly schooling — to maintain itself. Before this development schooling wasn't very important anywhere. We had it, but not too much of it, and only as much as an individual *wanted*. People learned to read, write, and do arithmetic just fine anyway; there are some studies that suggest literacy at the time of the American Revolution, at least for non-slaves on the Eastern seaboard, was close to total. Thomas Paine's *Common Sense* sold 600,000 copies to a population of 3,000,000, of whom twenty percent were slaves and fifty percent indentured servants.

Were the Colonists geniuses? No, the truth is that reading, writing, and arithmetic only take about one hundred hours to transmit as long as the audience is eager and willing to learn. The trick is to wait until someone asks and then move fast while the mood is on. Millions of people teach themselves these things — it really isn't very hard. Pick up a fifth-grade math or rhetoric textbook from 1850 and you'll see that the texts were pitched then on what would today be considered college level. The continuing cry for "basic skills" practice is a smoke screen behind which schools preempt the time of children for twelve years and teach them the seven lessons I've just described to you.

The society that has come increasingly under central control since just before the Civil War shows itself in the lives we lead, the clothes we wear, the food we eat, and the green highway signs we drive by from coast to coast, all of which are the products of this control. So too, I think, are the epidemics of drugs, suicide, divorce, violence, and cruelty, as well as the hardening of class into caste in the United States, products of the dehumanization of our lives, of the lessening of individual, family, and community importance — a diminishment that proceeds from central control. Inevitably, large compulsory institutions want more and more, until there isn't any more to give. School takes our children away from any possibility of an active role in community life — in fact, it destroys communities by relegating the training of children to the hands of certified experts — and by doing so it ensures our children cannot grow up fully human. Aristotle taught that without a fully active role in community life one could not hope to become a healthy human being. Surely he was right. Look around you the next time you are near a school or an old people's reservation if you wish a demonstration.

School, as it was built, is an essential support system for a model of social engineering that condemns most people to be subordinate stones in a pyramid that narrows as it ascends to a terminal of control. School is an artifice that makes such a pyramidical social order seem inevitable, even though such a premise is a fundamental betrayal of the American Revolution. From Colonial days through the period of the Republic we had no schools to speak of — read Benjamin Franklin's *Autobiography* for an example of a man who had no time to waste in school — and yet the promise of democracy was beginning to be realized. We turned our backs on this promise by bringing to life the ancient pharaonic dream of Egypt: compulsory subordination for all. That was the secret Plato reluctantly transmitted in *The Republic* when Glaucon and Adeimantus extort from Socrates the plan for total state control of human life, a plan necessary to maintain a society where some people take more than their share. "I will show you," says Socrates, "how to bring about such a feverish city, but you will not like what I am going to say." And so the blueprint of the seven-lesson school was first sketched.

The current debate about whether we should have a national curriculum is phony. We already have a national curriculum locked up in the seven lessons I have just outlined. Such a curriculum produces physical, moral, and intellectual paralysis, and no curriculum of content will be sufficient to reverse its hideous effects. What is currently under discussion in our national hysteria about failing academic performance misses the point. Schools teach exactly what they are intended to teach and they do it well: how to be a good Egyptian and remain in your place in the pyramid.

III

None of this is inevitable. None of it is impossible to overthrow. We do have choices in how we bring up young people: there is no one right way. If we broke through the power of the pyramidical illusion we would see that. There is no life-and-death international competition threatening our national existence, difficult as that idea is even to think about, let alone believe, in the face of a continual media barrage of myth to the contrary. In every important material respect our nation is self-sufficient, including in energy. I realize that idea runs counter to the most fashionable thinking of political economists, but the "profound transformation" of our economy these people talk about is neither inevitable nor irreversible.

Global economics does not speak to the public need for meaningful work, affordable housing, fulfilling education, adequate medical care, a clean environment, honest and accountable government, social and cultural renewal, or simple justice. All global ambitions are based on a definition of productivity and the good life so alienated from common human reality that I am convinced it is wrong and that most people would agree with me if they could perceive an alternative. We might be able to see that if we regained a hold on a philosophy that locates meaning where meaning is genuinely to be found — in families, in friends, in the passage of seasons, in nature, in simple ceremonies and rituals, in curiosity, generosity, compassion, and service to others, in a decent independence and privacy, in all the free and inexpensive things out of which real families, real friends, and real communities are built — then we would be so self-sufficient we would not even need the material "sufficiency" which our global "experts" are so insistent we be concerned about.

How did these awful places, these "schools," come about? Well, casual schooling has always been with us in a variety of forms, a mildly useful adjunct to growing up. But "modern schooling" as we now know it is a by-product of the two "Red Scares" of 1848 and 1919, when powerful interests feared a revolution among our own industrial poor. Partly, too, total schooling came about because old-line "American" families were appalled by the native cultures of Celtic, Slavic, and Latin immigrants of the 1840s and felt repugnance toward the Catholic religion they brought with them. Certainly a third contributing factor in creating a jail for children called "school" must have been the consternation with which these same "Americans" regarded the movement of African-Americans through the society in the wake of the Civil War.

Look again at the seven lessons of school teaching: confusion, class position, indifference, emotional and intellectual dependency, conditional self-esteem, and surveillance. All of these lessons are prime training for permanent underclasses, people deprived forever of finding the center of their own special genius. And over time this training has shaken loose from its original purpose: to regulate the poor. For since the 1920s the growth of the school bureaucracy as well as the less visible growth of a horde of industries that profit from schooling exactly as it is, has enlarged this institution's original grasp to the point that it now seizes the sons and daughters of the middle classes as well.

Is it any wonder Socrates was outraged at the accusation he took money to teach? Even then, philosophers saw clearly the inevitable direction the professionalization of teaching would take, that of preempting the teaching function, which, in a healthy community, belongs to everyone.

With lessons like the ones I teach day after day it should be little wonder we have a real national crisis, the nature of which is very different from that proclaimed by the national media. Young people are indifferent to the adult world and to the future, indifferent to almost everything except the diversion of toys and violence. Rich or poor, school children who face the twenty-first century cannot concentrate on anything for very long; they have a poor sense of time past and time to come. They are mistrustful of intimacy like the children of divorce they really are (for we have divorced them from significant parental attention); they hate solitude, are cruel, materialistic, dependent, passive, violent, timid in the face of the unexpected, addicted to distraction.

All the peripheral tendencies of childhood are nourished and magnified to a grotesque extent by schooling, which, through its hidden curriculum, prevents effective personality development. Indeed, without exploiting the fearfulness, selfishness, and inexperience of children, our schools could not survive at all, nor could I as a certified schoolteacher. No common school that actually dared to teach the use of critical thinking tools — like the dialectic, the heuristic, or other devices that free minds should employ — would last very long before being torn to pieces. In our secular society, school has become the replacement for church, and like church it requires that its teachings must be taken on faith.

It is time that we squarely face the fact that institutional schoolteaching is destructive to children. Nobody survives the seven-lesson curriculum completely unscathed, not even the instructors. The method is deeply and profoundly anti-educational. No tinkering will fix it. In one of the great ironies of human affairs, the massive rethinking the schools require would cost so much *less* than we are spending now that powerful interests cannot afford to let it happen. You must understand that first and foremost the business I am in is a *jobs project* and an agency for letting contracts. We cannot afford to save money by reducing the scope of our operation or by diversifying the product we offer, even to help children grow up right. That is the *iron law* of institutional schooling — it is a business, subject neither to normal accounting procedures nor to the rational scalpel of competition.

Some form of free-market system in public schooling is the likeliest place to look for answers, a free market where family schools and small entrepreneurial schools and religious schools and crafts schools and farm schools exist in profusion to compete with government education. I'm trying to describe a free market in schooling exactly like the one the country had until the Civil War, one in which *students volunteer for the kind of education that suits them* even if that means self-education. It didn't hurt Benjamin Franklin that I can see. These options exist now in miniature, wonderful survivals of a strong and vigorous past, but they are available only to the resourceful, the courageous, the lucky, or the rich. The near impossibility of one of these better roads opening for the shattered families of the poor or for the bewildered host camped on the fringes of the urban middle class suggests that *the disaster of seven-lesson schools is going to grow unless we do something bold and decisive with the mess of government monopoly schooling.*

After an adult lifetime spent teaching school, I believe the *method* of mass schooling is its only real content. Don't be fooled into thinking that good curriculum or good equipment or good teachers are the critical determinants of your son's or daughter's education. All the pathologies we've considered come about in large measure because the lessons of school prevent children from keeping important appointments with themselves and with their families to learn lessons in self-motivation, perseverance, self-reliance, courage, dignity, and love — and lessons in service to others, too, which are among the key lessons of home and community life.

Thirty years ago these lessons could still be learned in the time left *after* school. But television has eaten up most of that time, and a combination of television and the stresses peculiar to two-income or single-parent families has swallowed up most of what used to be family time as well. Our kids have no time left to grow up fully human and only thin-soil wastelands to do it in.

A future is rushing down upon our culture that will insist that all of us learn the wisdom of nonmaterial experience; a future that will demand as the price of survival that we follow a path of natural life that is economical in material cost. These lessons cannot be learned in schools as they are. School is a twelve-year jail sentence where bad habits are the only curriculum truly learned. I teach school and win awards doing it. I should know.

Chapter 2

THE PSYCHOPATHIC SCHOOL

This speech was given by the author on 31 January 1990 in accepting an award from the New York State Senate naming him New York City Teacher of the Year.

I ACCEPT THIS AWARD ON BEHALF of all the fine teachers I've known over the years who've struggled to make their transactions with children honorable ones, men and women who were never complacent, always questioning, always wrestling to define and redefine what the word "education" should mean. A Teacher of the Year is not the best teacher around (those people are too quiet to be easily uncovered), but she or he is a standard-bearer, representative of these private people who spend their lives gladly in the service of children. This is their award as well as mine.

I

We live in a time of great school crisis linked to an even greater social crisis. Our nation ranks at the bottom of nineteen industrial nations in reading, writing, and arithmetic. At the very bottom! The world's narcotic economy is based upon our consumption of this commodity; if we didn't buy so many powdered dreams, the business would collapse — and schools are an important sales outlet. Our teenage suicide rate is the highest in the world, and suicidal kids are rich kids for the most part, not the poor. In Manhattan, seventy percent of all new marriages last less than five years. So something is wrong for sure.

This great crisis that we witness in our schools is interlinked with a greater social crisis in the community. We seem to have lost our identity. Children and old people are penned up and locked away from the business of the world to a degree without precedent: nobody talks to them anymore, and without children and old people mixing in daily life, a community has no future and no past, only a continuous present. In fact, the term "community" hardly applies to the way we interact with each other. We live in *networks*, not communities, and everyone I know is lonely because of that. School is a major actor in this tragedy, as it is a major actor in the widening gulf among social classes. Using school as a sorting mechanism, we appear to be on the way to creating a caste system, complete with untouchables who wander through subway trains begging and who sleep upon the streets.

I've noticed a fascinating phenomenon in my thirty years of teaching: schools and schooling are increasingly irrelevant to the great enterprises of the planet. No one believes anymore that scientists are trained in science classes or politicians in civics classes or poets in English classes. The truth is that schools don't really teach anything except how to obey orders. This is a great mystery to me because thousands of humane, caring people work in schools as teachers and aides and administrators, but the abstract logic of the institution overwhelms their individual contributions. Although teachers do care and do work very, very hard, the institution is psychopathic — it has no conscience. It rings a bell and the young man in the middle of writing a poem must close his notebook and move to a different cell where he must memorize that humans and monkeys derive from a common ancestor.

II

Our form of compulsory schooling is an invention of the State of Massachusetts around 1850. It was resisted — sometimes with guns — by an estimated eighty percent of the Massachusetts population, the last outpost in Barnstable on Cape Cod not surrendering its children until the 1880s, when the area was seized by militia and children marched to school under guard.

Now here is a curious idea to ponder: Senator Ted Kennedy's office released a paper not too long ago claiming that *prior* to compulsory education the state literacy rate was ninety-eight percent and that after it the figure never exceeded ninety-one percent, where it stands in 1990.

Here is another curiosity to think about: The home-schooling movement has quietly grown to a size where one and half million young people are being educated entirely by their own parents; last month the education press reported the amazing news that, in their ability to think, children schooled at home seem to be five or even ten years ahead of their formally trained peers.

III

I don't think we'll get rid of schools any time soon, certainly not in my lifetime, but if we're going to change what's rapidly becoming a disaster of ignorance, we need to realize that the school institution "schools" very well, though it does not "educate" — that's inherent in the design of the thing. It's not the fault of bad teachers or too little money spent. It's just impossible for education and schooling ever to be the same thing.

Schools were designed by Horace Mann and by Sears and Harper of the University of Chicago and by Thorndyke of Columbia Teachers College and by some other men to be instruments for the scientific management of a mass population. Schools are intended to produce, through the application of formulas, formulaic human beings whose behavior can be predicted and controlled.

To a very great extent schools succeed in doing this, but in a national order increasingly disintegrated, in a national order in which the only "successful" people are independent, self-reliant, confident, and individualistic (because community life which protects the dependent and the weak is dead and only networks remain), the products of schooling are, as I've said, irrelevant. Well-schooled people are irrelevant. They can sell film and razor blades, push paper and talk on telephones, or sit mindlessly before a flickering computer terminal, but as human beings they are useless. Useless to others and useless to themselves.

The daily misery around us is, I think, in large measure caused by the fact that, as Paul Goodman put it thirty years ago, we force children to grow up absurd. Any reform in schooling has to deal with its absurdities.

It is absurd and anti-life to be part of a system that compels you to sit in confinement with people of exactly the same age and social class. That system effectively cuts you off from the immense diversity of life and the synergy of variety; indeed, it cuts you off from your own past and future, sealing you in a continuous present much the same way television does.

It is absurd and anti-life to move from cell to cell at the sound of a gong for every day of your natural youth in an institution that allows you no privacy and even follows you into the sanctuary of your home, demanding that you do its "homework."

"How will they learn to read?" you ask, and my answer is "Remember the lessons of Massachusetts." When children are given whole lives instead of age-graded ones in cellblocks they learn to read, write, and do arithmetic with ease, *if* those things make sense in the kind of life that unfolds around them.

But keep in mind that in the United States almost nobody who reads, writes, or does arithmetic gets much respect. We are a land of talkers; we pay talkers the most and admire talkers the most and so our children talk constantly, following the public models of television and schoolteachers. It is very difficult to teach the "basics" anymore because they really aren't basic to the society we've made.

IV

Two institutions at present control our children's lives: television and schooling, in that order. Both of these reduce the real world of wisdom, fortitude, temperance, and justice to a never-ending, nonstop abstraction. In centuries past, the time of childhood and adolescence would have been occupied in real work, real charity, real adventures, and the realistic search for mentors who might teach what you really wanted to learn. A great deal of time was spent in community pursuits, practicing affection, meeting and studying every level of the community, learning how to make a home, and dozens of other tasks necessary to becoming a whole man or woman.

But here is the calculus of time the children I teach must deal with:

Out of the 168 hours in each week my children sleep 56. That leaves them 112 hours a week out of which to fashion a self.

According to recent reports, children watch 55 hours of television a week. That then leaves them 57 hours a week in which to grow up.

My children attend school 30 hours a week, use about eight hours getting ready for and traveling to and from school, and spend an average of seven hours a week in homework — a total of 45 hours. During that time they are under constant surveillance. They have no private time or private space and are disciplined if they try to assert individuality in the use of time or space. That leaves them 12 hours a week out of which to create a unique consciousness. Of course my kids eat, too, and that takes some time — not much because they've lost the tradition of family dining — but if we allot three hours a week to evening meals, we arrive at a net amount of private time for each child of nine hours per week.

It's not enough, is it? The richer the kid, of course, the less television he or she watches, but the rich kid's time is just as narrowly prescribed by a somewhat broader catalogue of commercial entertainments and the inevitable assignment to a series of private lessons in areas seldom of his or her own choice.

But these activities are just a more cosmetic way to create dependent human beings, unable to fill their own hours, unable to initiate lines of meaning to give substance and pleasure to their existence. It's a national disease, this dependency and aimlessness, and I think schooling and television and lessons have a lot to do with it.

Think of the phenomena which are killing us as a nation: narcotic drugs, brainless competition, recreational sex, the pornography of violence, gambling, and alcohol — and the worst pornography of all: lives devoted to buying things, accumulation as a philosophy. All of these are addictions of dependent personalities, and this is what our brand of schooling must inevitably produce.

V

I want to tell you what the effect on our children is of us taking all their time from them — time they need to grow up — and forcing them to spend it on abstractions. You need to hear this because any reform that doesn't attack these specific pathologies will be nothing more than a facade.

1. The children I teach are indifferent to the adult world. This defies the experience of thousands of years. A close study of what big people were up to was always the most exciting occupation of youth, but nobody wants children to grow up these days, least of all the children themselves — and who can blame them? *Toys are us.*

2. The children I teach have almost no curiosity, and what little they do have is transitory. They cannot concentrate for very long, even on things they choose to do. Can you see a connection between the bells ringing again and again to change classes and this phenomenon of evanescent attention?

3. The children I teach have a poor sense of the future, of how tomorrow is inextricably linked to today. As I said before, they live in a continuous present: the exact moment they are in is the boundary of their consciousness.

4. The children I teach are ahistorical: they have no sense of how the past has predestinated their own present, limits their choices, shapes their values and lives.

5. The children I teach are cruel to each other; they lack compassion for misfortune; they laugh at weakness; they have contempt for people whose need for help shows too plainly.

6. The children I teach are uneasy with intimacy or candor. They cannot deal with genuine intimacy because of a lifelong habit of preserving a secret inner self inside a larger outer personality made up of artificial bits and pieces of behavior borrowed from television or acquired to manipulate teachers. Because they are not who they represent themselves to be, the disguise wears thin in the presence of intimacy; so intimate relationships have to be avoided.

7. The children I teach are materialistic, following the lead of schoolteachers who materialistically "grade everything" and of television mentors who offer everything in the world for sale.

8. The children I teach are dependent, passive, and timid in the presence of new challenges. This timidity is frequently masked by surface bravado or by anger or aggressiveness, but underneath is a vacuum without fortitude.

I could name a few other conditions that school reform will have to tackle if our national decline is to be arrested, but by now you will have grasped my thesis, whether you agree with it or not. Either schools have caused these pathologies, or television has, or both. It's a simple matter of arithmetic: between schooling and television, all the time the children have is eaten up. There simply isn't enough other time in the experience of our kids for there to be other significant causes.

VI

What can be done?

First, we need a ferocious national debate that doesn't quit, day after day, year after year, the kind of continuous debate that journalism finds boring. We need to scream and argue about this school thing until it is fixed or broken beyond repair, one or the other. If we can fix it, fine; if we cannot, then the success of home-schooling shows a different road that has great promise. Pouring the money we now pour into schooling back into family education might cure two ailments with one medicine, repairing families as it repairs children.

Genuine reform is possible, but it shouldn't cost anything. More money and more people pumped into this sick institution will only make it sicker. We need to rethink the fundamental premises of schooling and decide *what* it is we want all children to learn and *why*. For 140 years this nation has tried to impose objectives downward from a lofty command center made up of "experts," a central elite of social engineers. It hasn't worked. It won't work. And it is a gross betrayal of the democratic promise that once made this nation a noble experiment. The Russian attempt to create Plato's republic in Eastern Europe has exploded before our eyes; our own attempt to impose the same sort of central orthodoxy using the schools as an instrument is also coming apart at the seams, albeit more slowly and painfully. It doesn't work because its fundamental premises are mechanical, antihuman, and hostile to family life. Lives can be controlled by machine education, but they will always fight back with weapons of social pathology: drugs, violence, self-destruction, indifference, and the symptoms I see in the children I teach.

VII

It's high time we looked backwards to regain an educational philosophy that works. One I like particularly well has been a favorite of the ruling classes of Europe for thousands of years. I use as much of it as I can manage in my own teaching, as much, that is, as I can get away with, given the present institution of compulsory schooling. I think it works just as well for poor children as for rich ones.

At the core of this elite system of education is the belief that self-knowledge is the only basis of true knowledge. Everywhere in this system, at every age, you will find arrangements that work to place the child *alone* in an unguided setting with a problem to solve. Sometimes the problem is fraught with great risks, such as the problem of galloping a horse or making it jump, but that, of course, is a problem successfully solved by thousands of elite children before the age of ten. Can you imagine anyone who had mastered such a challenge ever lacking confidence in his ability to do anything? Sometimes the problem is the problem of mastering solitude, as Thoreau did at Walden Pond, or Einstein did in the Swiss customs house.

Right now we are taking from our children all the time that they need to develop self-knowledge. That has to stop. We have to invent school experiences that give a lot of that time back. We need to trust children from a very early age with independent study, perhaps arranged in school, but which takes place *away* from the institutional setting. We need to invent curricula where each kid has a chance to develop private uniqueness and self-reliance.

A short time ago I took $70 and sent a twelve-year-old girl from my class, with her non-English-speaking mother, on a bus down the New Jersey coast to take the police chief of Seabright to lunch and apologize for polluting his beach with a discarded Gatorade bottle. In exchange for this public apology I had arranged with the police chief for the girl to have a one-day apprenticeship in small-town police procedures. A few days later two more of my twelve-year-old kids traveled alone from Harlem to West Thirty-first street where they began an apprenticeship with a newspaper editor; later three of my kids found themselves in the middle of the Jersey swamps at six in the morning, studying the mind of a trucking company president as he dispatched eighteen-wheelers to Dallas, Chicago, and Los Angeles.

Are these "special" children in a "special" program? Well, in one sense yes, but nobody knows about this program except I and the kids. They're just nice kids from central Harlem, bright and alert, but so badly schooled when they came to me that most of them couldn't add or subtract with any fluency. And not a single one knew the population of New York City or how far New York is from California.

Does that worry me? Of course! But I am confident that as they gain self-knowledge they'll also become self-teachers — and only self-teaching has any lasting value.

We've got to give kids independent time right away because that is the key to self-knowledge, and we must reinvolve them with the real world as fast as possible so that their independent time can be spent on something other than abstraction. This is an emergency — it requires drastic action to correct.

VIII

What else does a restructured school system need? It needs to stop being a parasite on the working community. Of all the pages in the human ledger, only our tortured country has warehoused children and asked nothing of them in service of the general good. For a while I think we need to make community service a required part of schooling. Besides the experience of acting unselfishly that it will teach, it is the quickest way to give young children real responsibility in the mainstream of life.

For five years I ran a guerrilla school program where I had every kid, rich and poor, smart and dipsy, give 320 hours a year of hard community service. Dozens of those kids came back to me years later, grown up, and told me that the experience of helping someone else had changed their lives. It had taught them to see in new ways, to rethink goals and values. It happened when they were thirteen, in my Lab School program, and was only possible because my rich school district was in chaos. When "stability" returned, the Lab closed. It was too successful with a widely mixed group of kids, at too small a cost, to be allowed to continue.

Independent study, community service, adventures and experience, large doses of privacy and solitude, a thousand different apprenticeships — the one-day variety or longer — these are all powerful, cheap, and effective ways to start a real reform of schooling. But no large-scale reform is ever going to work to repair our damaged children and our damaged society until we force open the idea of "school" to include *family* as the main engine of education. If we use schooling to break children away from parents — and make no mistake, that has been the central function of schools since John Cotton announced it as the purpose of the Bay Colony schools in 1650 and Horace Mann announced it as the purpose of Massachusetts schools in 1850 — we're going to continue to have the horror show we have right now.

The "Curriculum of Family" is at the heart of any good life. We've gotten away from that curriculum — it's time to return to it. The way to sanity in education is for our schools to take the lead in releasing the stranglehold of institutions on family life, to promote during schooltime confluences of parent and child that will strengthen family bonds. That was my real purpose in sending the girl and her mother down the Jersey coast to meet the police chief.

I have many ideas for formulating a family curriculum and my guess is that a lot of you have many ideas, too. Our greatest problem in getting the kind of grassroots thinking going that could reform schooling is that we have large vested interests preempting all the air time and profiting from schooling as it is, despite their rhetoric to the contrary.

We have to demand that new voices and new ideas get a hearing: my ideas and yours. We've all had a bellyful of authorized voices mediated by television and the press — a decade-long free-for-all debate is what is called for now, not any more "expert" opinions. Experts in education have never been right; their "solutions" are expensive and self-serving and always involve further centralization. We've seen the results.

It's time for a return to democracy, individuality, and family.

Chapter

3

THE GREEN
MONONGAHELA

*Awarded First Prize, Geraldine Dodge Foundation
— Columbia University National Essay Contest.*

IN THE BEGINNING I BECAME a teacher without realiz-
ing it. At the time, I was growing up on the banks of
the green Monongahela River forty miles southwest of
Pittsburgh, and on the banks of that deep green and
always mysterious river I became a student too, master
of the flight patterns of blue dragonflies and cunning
adversary of the iridescent ticks that infested the riverbank willows.

"Mind you watch the ticks, Jackie!" Grandmother
Mossie would call as I headed for the riverbank, summer
and winter, only a two-minute walk from Second Street,
where I lived across the trolley tracks of Main Street and
the Pennsylvania Railroad tracks that paralleled them. I
watched the red and yellow ticks chewing holes in the
pale green leaves as I ran to the riverbank. On the river I
drank my first Iron City at eight, smoked every cigarette
obtainable, and watched dangerous men and women

make love there at night on blankets all before I was twelve. It was my laboratory: I learned to watch closely and draw conclusions there.

How did the river make me a teacher? Listen. It was alive with paddle-wheel steamers in center channel, the turning paddles churning up clouds of white spray, making the green river boil bright orange where its chemical undercurrent was troubled; from shore you could clearly hear the loud *thump thump thump* on the water. From all over town young boys ran gazing in awe. A dozen times a day. No one ever became indifferent to these steamers because nothing important can ever really be boring. You can see the difference, can't you, between those serious boats and the truly boring space-craft of the past few decades, just flying junk without a purpose a boy can believe in? It's hard to feign an interest even now that I teach for a living and would like to pretend for the sake of the New York kids who won't have paddle-wheelers in their lives. The rockets are dull toys children in Manhattan put aside the day after Christmas, never to be touched again; the riverboats were serious magic, clearly demarcating the world of boys from the world of men. Lévi-Strauss would know how to explain.

In Monongahela by that river everyone was my teacher. Daily, it seemed to a boy, one of the mile-long trains would stop in town to take on water and coal, or for some mysterious reason; the brakeman and engineer would step among snot-nosed kids and spin railroad yarns, let us run in and out of boxcars, over and under flat-cars, tank cars, coal cars, and numbers of other specialty

cars whose function we memorized as easily as we memorized enemy plane silhouettes. Once a year, maybe, we
got taken into the caboose that reeked of stale beer to be
offered a bologna-on-white-bread sandwich. The anonymous men lectured, advised, and inspired the boys of
Monongahela — that was as much their job as driving
the trains.

Sometimes a riverboat would stop in mid-channel
and discharge a crew who would row to shore, tying
their skiff to one of the willows. That was the excuse for
every rickety skiff in the twelve-block-long town to fill
up with kids, pulling like Vikings, sometimes with sticks
instead of oars, to raid the "Belle of Pittsburgh" or "The
Original River Queen." Some kind of natural etiquette
was at work in Monongahela. The rules didn't need to
be written down; if men had time they showed boys how
to grow up. We didn't whine when our time was up:
men had work to do — we understood that and scam-
pered away, grateful for the flash of our own futures they
had had time to reveal, however small it was.

I was arrested three times growing up in
Monongahela or, rather, picked up by the police and
taken to jail to await a visit from Pappy to spring me. I
wouldn't trade those times for anything. The first time
I was nine, caught on my belly under a parked car at
night, half an hour after curfew; in 1943, blinds were
always drawn in the Monongahela Valley for fear that
Hitler's planes would somehow find a way to reach
across the Atlantic to our steel mills lining both banks of
the river. The Nazis were apparently waiting for a wor-
ried mother to go searching for her child with a

flashlight after curfew, then *whammo!* down would swoop the Teutonic air fleet!

Charlie was the cop's name. Down to the lockup we went — no call to mother until Charlie had diagrammed the deadly menace of Goering's Luftwaffe. What a geopolitics lesson that was! Another time I speared a goldfish in the town fishpond and was brought from jail to the library, where I was sentenced to read for a month about the lives of animals. Finally, on V-J Day — when the Japanese cried "Uncle!" — I accepted a dare and broke the window of the police cruiser with a slingshot. Confessing, I suffered my first encounter with employment to pay for the glass, becoming sweep-up boy in my grandfather's printing office at fifty cents a week.

After I went away to Cornell I saw Monongahela and its green river only one more time: when I went there after my freshman year to give blood to my dying grandfather, who lay in the town hospital, as strong in his dying as he had ever been in his living. In another room my grandmother lay dying. Both passed within twenty-four hours, my granddad, Harry Taylor Zimmer, Sr., taking my blood to his grave in the cemetery there. My family moved again and again and again, but in my own heart I never left Monongahela, where I learned to teach from being taught by everyone in town, where I learned to teach the love of work from being asked to shoulder my share of responsibility, even as a boy, and where I learned to find adventures I made myself from the everyday stuff around me — the river and the people who lived alongside it.

In 1964, I was making a lot of money. That's what I walked away from to become a teacher. I was a copywriter on the fast track in advertising, a young fellow with a knack for writing thirty-second television commercials. My work required about one full day a month to complete, the rest of the time being spent in power breakfasts, after-work martinis at Michael's Pub, keeping up with the shifting fortunes of about twenty agencies in order to gauge the right time to jump ship for more money, and endless parties that always seemed to culminate in colossal headaches.

It bothered me that all the urgencies of the job were generated externally, but it bothered me more that the work I was doing seemed to have very little importance — even to the people who were paying for it. Worst of all, the problems this work posed were cut from such a narrow spectrum that it was clear that past, present, and future were to be of a piece: a twenty-nine-year-old man's work was no different from a thirty-nine-year-old man's work or a forty-nine-year-old man's work (though there didn't seem to be any forty-nine-year-old copywriters — I had no idea why not).

"I'm leaving," I said one day to the copy chief.

"Are you nuts, Jack? You'll get profit sharing this year. We can match any offer you've got. Leaving for who?"

"For nobody, Dan. I mean I'm going to teach junior high school."

"When you see your mother next, tell her for me she raised a moron. Christ! Are you going to be sorry! In New York City we don't have schools; we have pens for lost souls. Teaching is a scam, a welfare project for losers who can't do anything else!"

Round and round I went with my advertising colleagues for a few days. Their scorn only firmed my resolve; the riverboats and trains of Monongahela were working inside me. I needed something to do that wasn't absurd more than I needed another party or a new abstract number in my bankbook.

And so I became a junior high school substitute teacher, working the beat from what's now Lincoln Center to Columbia, my alma mater, and from Harlem to the South Bronx. After three months the dismal working conditions, the ugly rooms, the torn books, the repeated instances of petty complaints from authorities, the bells, the buzzers, the drab teacher food in the cafeterias, the unpressed clothing, the inexplicable absence of conversation about children among the teachers (to this day, after thirty years in the business, I can honestly say I have *never once* heard an extended conversation about children or about teaching theory in any teachers' room I've been in) had just about done me in.

In fact, on the very first day I taught I was attacked by a boy waving a chair above his head. It happened in the infamous junior high school Wadleigh, on 113th Street. I was given the eighth grade typing class — seventy-five students and typewriters — with this one injunction: "Under no circumstances are you to allow them to type. You lack the proper license. Is that understood?" A man named Mr. Bash said that to me.

It couldn't have taken more than sixty seconds from the time I closed the door and issued the order not to type for one hundred and fifty hands to snake under the typewriter covers and begin to type. But not all at once — that would have been too easy. First, three machines began to *clack clack* from the right rear. Quick, who were the culprits? I would race to the corner, screaming *stop!* when suddenly, behind my back, three other machines would begin! Whirling as only a young man can do, I caught one small boy in the act. Then, to a veritable symphony of machines clicking, bells ringing, platens being thrown, I hoisted the boy from his chair and announced at the top of my foolish lungs I would make an example of this miscreant.

"Look out!" a girl shouted, and I turned toward her voice just in time to see a large brother of the little fellow I held heading toward me with a chair raised above his head. Releasing his brother, I seized a chair myself and raised it aloft. A standoff! We regarded each other at a distance of about ten feet for what seemed forever, the class jeering and howling, when the room door opened and Assistant Principal Bash, the very man who'd given the no-typing order, appeared.

"Mr. Gatto, have these children been typing?"

"No, sir," I said, lowering my chair, "but I think they want to. What do you suggest they do instead?"

He looked at me for signs of impudence or insubordination for a second, then, as if thinking better of rebuking this upstart, he said merely, "Fall back on your resources," and left the room.

Most of the kids laughed — they'd seen this drama enacted before.

The situation was defused, but silently I dubbed Wadleigh the "Death School." Stopping by the office on my way home, I told the secretary not to call me again if they needed a sub.

The very next morning my phone rang at 6:30. "Are you available for work today, Mr. Gatto?" said the voice briskly.

"Who is this?" I asked suspiciously. (Ten schools were using me for sub work in those days, and each identified itself at once.)

"The law clearly states, Mr. Gatto, that we do not have to tell you who we are until you tell us whether you are available for work."

"Never mind," I bellowed, "there's only one school who'd pull such crap! The answer is *no!* I am never available to work in your pigpen school!" And I slammed the receiver back onto its cradle.

But the truth was none of the sub assignments were boat rides: schools had an uncanny habit of exploiting substitutes and providing no support for their survival. It's likely I'd have returned to advertising if a little girl, desperate to free herself from an intolerable situation, hadn't drawn me into her personal school nightmare and shown me how I could find my own significance in teaching, just as those strong men in the riverboats and trains had found their own significance, a currency all of us need for our self-esteem.

It happened this way. Occasionally I'd get a call from an elementary school. This particular day it was a third grade assignment at a school on 107th Street, which in those days was nearly one hundred percent non-Hispanic in its teaching staff and 99% Hispanic in its student body.

Like many desperate teachers, I lolled most of the

day listening to the kids read, one after another, and expending most of my energy trying to shut the audience up. This class had a very low ranking, and no one was able to put more than three or four words together without stumbling. All of a sudden, though, a little girl named Milagros sailed through a selection without a mistake. After class I called her over to my desk and asked why she was in this class of bad readers. She replied that "they" (the administration) wouldn't let her out because, as they explained to her mother, she was really a bad reader who had fantasies of being a better reader than she was. "But look, Mr. Gatto, my brother is in the sixth grade, and I can read every word in his English book better than he can!"

I was a little intrigued, but truthfully not much. Surely the authorities knew what they were doing. Still, the little girl seemed so frustrated I invited her to calm down and read to me from the sixth grade book. I explained that if she did well, I would take her case to the principal. I expected nothing.

Milagros, on the other hand, expected justice. Diving into "The Devil and Daniel Webster," she polished off the first two pages without a gulp. My God, I thought, this is a real reader. What is she doing here? Well, maybe it was a simple accident, easily corrected. I sent her home, promising to argue her case. Little did I suspect what a hornet's nest my request to have Milagros moved to a better class would stir up.

"You have some nerve, Mr. Gatto. I can't remember when a substitute ever told me how to run my school before. Have you taken specialized courses in reading?"

"No."

"Well then, suppose you leave these matters to the experts!"

"But the kid can *read*!"

"What do you suggest?"

"I suggest you test her, and if she isn't a dummy, get her out of the class she's in!"

"I don't like your tone. None of our children are dummies, Mr. Gatto. And you will find that girls like Milagros have many ways to fool amateurs like yourself. This is a matter of a child having memorized one story. You can see if I had to waste my time arguing with people like you, I'd have no time left to run a school."

But, strangely, I felt self-appointed as the girl's champion, even though I'd probably never see her again.

I insisted, and the principal finally agreed to test Milagros herself the following Wednesday after school. I made it a point to tell the little girl the next day. By that time I'd come to think that the principal was probably right — she'd memorized one story — but I still warned her she'd need to know the vocabulary from the whole advanced reader and be able to read any story the principal picked, without hesitation. My responsibility was over, I told myself.

The following Wednesday after school I waited in the room for Milagros' ordeal to be over. At 3:30 she shyly opened the door of the room.

"How'd it go?" I asked.

"I don't know," she answered, "but I didn't make any mistakes. Mrs. Hefferman was very angry, I could tell."

I saw Mrs. Hefferman, the principal, early the next morning before school opened. "It seems we've made a mistake with Milagros," she said curtly. "She will be moved, Mr. Gatto. Her mother has been informed."

Several weeks later, when I got back to the school to sub, Milagros dropped by, telling me she was in the fast class now and doing very well. She also gave me a sealed card. When I got home that night, I found it, unopened, in my suitcoat pocket. I opened it and saw a gaudy birthday card with blue flowers on it. Opening the card, I read, "A teacher like you cannot be found. Signed. Your student, Milagros."

That simple sentence made me a teacher for life. It was the first praise I'd ever heard in my working existence that had any meaning. I never forgot it, though I never saw Milagros again and only heard of her again in 1988, twenty-four years later. Then one day I picked up a newspaper and read:

Occupational Teacher Award

Milagros M., United Federation of Teachers, has won the Distinguished Occupational Teacher Award of the State Education Department for "demonstrated achievement and exemplary professionalism." A secretarial studies teacher at Norman Thomas High School, New York City, from which she graduated, Miss M. was selected as a Manhattan Teacher of the Year in 1985 and was nominated the following year for the Woman of Conscience Award given by the National Council of Women.

Ah, Milagros, is it just possible that I was your Monongahela River? No matter, a teacher like you cannot be found.

Chapter

4

WE NEED LESS SCHOOL, NOT MORE

"We were making the future," he said, and hardly any
of us troubled to think what future we were making.
And here it is!
— *The Sleeper Awakes*, H. G. Wells

*This essay — a personal favorite — was written especially for the first edition,
and presented many times as a public speech before the book was published.*

I

A SURPRISING NUMBER OF otherwise sensible people
find it hard to see why the scope and reach of our
formal schooling networks should not be increased (by
extending the school day or year, for instance) in order
to provide an economical solution to the problems
posed by the decay of the American family. One reason
for their preference, I think, is that they have trouble
understanding the real difference between communities
and networks, or even the difference between families
and networks.

Because of this confusion they conclude that replacing a bad network with a good one is the right way to go. Since I disagree so strongly with the fundamental premise that networks are workable substitutes for families, and because from anybody's point of view a lot more school is going to cost a lot more money, I thought I'd tell you why, from a school teacher's perspective, we shouldn't be thinking of more school, but of *less*.

People who admire our school institution usually admire networking in general and have an easy time seeing its positive side, but they overlook its negative aspect: networks, even good ones, drain the vitality from communities and families. They provide *mechanical* ("by-the-numbers") solutions to human problems, when a slow, organic process of self-awareness, self-discovery, and cooperation is what is required if any solution is to stick.

Think of the challenge of losing weight. It's possible to employ mechanical tricks to do this quickly, but I'm told that ninety-five percent of the poor souls who do are only fooling themselves. The weight lost this way doesn't stay off; it comes back in a short time. Other network solutions are just as temporary: a group of law students may network to pass their college exams, but preparing a brief in private practice is often a solitary, lonely experience.

Aristotle saw, a long time ago, that fully participating in a complex range of human affairs was the only way to be become fully human; in *that* he differed from Plato. What is gained from consulting a specialist and surrendering all judgment is often more than outweighed by a permanent loss of one's own volition. This discovery accounts for the curious texture of *real* communication, where people argue with their doctors, lawyers, and ministers, tell craftsmen what they want instead of accepting what they get, frequently make their own food from scratch instead of buying it in a restaurant or defrosting it, and perform many similar acts of *participation*. A real community is, of course, a collection of real families who themselves function in this participatory way.

Networks, however, don't require the whole person, but only a narrow piece. If, on the other hand, you function in a network, it asks you to suppress all the parts of yourself except the network-interest part — a highly unnatural act although one you can get used to. In exchange, the network will deliver efficiency in the pursuit of some limited aim. This is, in fact, a devil's bargain, since on the promise of some future gain one must surrender the wholeness of one's present humanity. If you enter into too many of these bargains, you will split yourself into many specialized pieces, none of them completely human. And no time is available to reintegrate them. This, ironically, is the destiny of many successful networkers and doubtless generates much business for divorce courts and therapists of a variety of persuasions.

The fragmentation caused by excessive networking creates diminished humanity, a sense that our lives are out of control — because they are. If we face the present school and community crisis squarely, with hopes of finding a better way, we need to accept that schools, as networks, create a large part of the agony of modem life. We don't need more schooling — we need less.

I expect you'll want some proof of that, even though the million or so people participating in education at home these days have begun to nibble at the edge of everybody's consciousness and promise to bite their way into national attention when details of their success get around a little more. So for those of you who haven't heard that you don't need officially certified teachers in officially certified schools to get a good education, let me try to expose some of the machinery that makes certified schooling so bad. And remember, if you're thinking, "but it's *always* been that way" — it really hasn't.

Compulsory schooling in factory schools is a very recent, very Massachusetts/New York development. Remember, too, that until thirty odd years ago you could escape mass schooling *after* school; now it is much harder to escape because another form of mass schooling — television — has spread all over the place to blot up any attention spared by school. So what was merely grotesque in our national treatment of the young before 1960 has become tragic now that mass commercial entertainment, as addictive as any other hallucinogenic drug, has blocked the escape routes from mass schooling.

It is a fact generally ignored when considering the communal nature of institutional families like schools, large corporations, colleges, armies, hospitals, and government agencies that they are not real communities at all, but networks. Unlike communities, networks, as I reminded you, have a very narrow way of allowing people to associate, and that way is always across a short spectrum of one, or at most a few, specific uniformities.

In spite of ritual moments like the Christmas party or the office softball game — when individual human components in the network "go home," they go home alone. And in spite of humanitarian support from fellow workers that eases emergencies — when people in networks suffer, they suffer alone, unless they have a family or community to suffer with them.

Even with college dorm "communities," those most engaging and intimate simulations of community imaginable, who among us has not experienced the awful realization after graduation that we cannot remember our friends' names or faces very well? Or who, if we can remember, feels much desire to renew those associations?

It is a puzzling development, as yet poorly understood, that the "caring" in networks is in some important way feigned. Not maliciously, but in spite of any genuine emotional attractions that might be there, human behavior in network situations often resembles a dramatic act — matching a script produced to meet the demands of a story. And, as such, the intimate moments in networks lack the sustaining value of their counterparts in community. Those of you who remember the wonderful closeness possible in army camp life or sports teams and who have now forgotten those you were once close with will understand what I mean. In contrast, have you ever forgotten an uncle or an aunt?

If the loss of true community entailed by masquerading in networks is not noticed in time, a condition arises in the victim's spirit very much like the "trout starvation" that used to strike wilderness explorers whose diet was made up exclusively of stream fish. While trout quell the pangs of hunger — and even taste good — the eater gradually suffers for want of sufficient nutrients.

Networks like schools are not communities, just as school training is not education. By preempting fifty percent of the total time of the young, by locking young people up with other young people exactly their own age, by ringing bells to start and stop work, by asking people to think about the same thing at the same time in the same way, by grading people the way we grade vegetables — and in a dozen other vile and stupid ways — network schools steal the vitality of communities and replace it with an ugly mechanism. No one survives these places with their humanity intact, not kids, not teachers, not administrators, and not parents.

A community is a place in which people face each other over time in *all* their human variety: good parts, bad parts, and all the rest. Such places promote the highest quality of life possible — lives of engagement and participation. This happens in unexpected ways, but it never happens when you've spent more than a decade listening to other people *talk* and trying to do what they tell you to do, trying to *please* them after the fashion of schools. It makes a real lifelong difference whether you avoid that training or it traps you.

An example might clarify this. Networks of urban reformers will convene to consider the problems of homeless vagrants, but a community will think of its vagrants as real people, not abstractions. Ron, Dave or Marty — a community will call its bums by their names. It makes a difference.

People interact on thousands of invisible pathways in a community, and the emotional payoff is correspondingly rich and complex. But networks can only manage a cartoon simulation of community and provide a very limited payoff.

I belong to some networks myself, of course, but the only ones I consider completely safe are the ones that reject their communal facade, acknowledge their limits, and concentrate solely on helping me do a specific and necessary task. But a vampire network like a school, which tears off huge chunks of time and energy needed for building community and family — and always asks for *more* — needs to have a stake driven through its heart and be nailed into its coffin. The feeding frenzy of formal schooling has already wounded us seriously in our ability to form families and communities, by bleeding away time we need with our children and our children need with us. That's why I say we need less school, not more.

Who can deny that networks can get some jobs done? They do. But they lack any ability to nourish their members emotionally. The extreme *rationality* at the core of networking is based on the same misperception of human nature the French Enlightenment and Comte were guilty of. At our best we human beings are much, much grander than merely rational; at our best we transcend rationality while incorporating its procedures into our lower levels of functioning. This is why computers will never replace people, for they are condensed to be rational, and hence very limited.

Networks divide people, first from themselves and then from each other, on the grounds that this is the efficient way to perform a task. It may well be, but it is a lousy way to feel good about being alive. Networks make people lonely. They cannot correct their inhuman mechanism and still succeed as networks. Behind the anomaly that networks look like communities (but are not) lurks the grotesque secret of mass schooling and the reason why enlarging the school domain will only aggravate the dangerous conditions of social disintegration it is intended to correct.

I want to repeat this until you are sick of hearing it. Networks do great harm by appearing enough like real communities to create expectations that they can manage human social and psychological needs. The reality is that they cannot. Even associations as inherently harmless as bridge clubs, chess clubs, amateur acting groups, or groups of social activists will, if they maintain a pretense of whole friendship, ultimately produce that odd sensation familiar to all city dwellers of being lonely in the middle of a crowd. Which of us who frequently networks has not felt this sensation? Belonging to many networks does *not* add up to having a community, no matter how many you belong to or how often your telephone rings.

With a network, what you get at the beginning is all you ever get. Networks don't get better or worse; their limited purpose keeps them pretty much the same all the time, as there just isn't much development possible. The pathological state which eventually develops out of these constant repetitions of thin human contact is a feeling that your "friends" and "colleagues" don't really care about you beyond what you can do for them, that they have no curiosity about the way you manage your life, no curiosity about your hopes, fears, victories, defeats. The real truth is that the "friends" falsely mourned for their indifference were never friends, just fellow networkers from whom in fairness little should be expected beyond attention to the common interest.

But given our unquenchable need for community and the unlikelihood of obtaining that community in a network, we are so desperate for any solution that we are driven to deceive ourselves about the nature of these liaisons. Whatever "caring" really means, it means something more than simple companionship or even the comradeship of shared interests.

II

In the growth of human society, families came first, communities second, and only much later came the institutions set up by the community to serve it. Most institutional rhetoric — the proclaiming of what is important — borrows its values from those of individual families that work well together.

Particularly over the past century and a half in the United States, spokesmen for institutional life have demanded a role above and beyond service to families and communities. They have sought to command and prescribe as kings used to do, though there is an important difference. In the case of ancient kings, once beyond the range of their voices and trumpets you could usually do what you pleased; but in the case of modem institutions, the reach of technology is everywhere — there is no escape if the place where you live and the family you live in cannot provide sanctuary.

Institutions, say their political philosophers, are better at creating marching orders for the human race than families are; therefore they should no longer be expected to follow but should lead. Institutional leaders have come to regard themselves as great *synthetic fathers* to millions of *synthetic children*, by which I mean to all of us. This theory sees us bound together in some abstract family relationship in which the state is the true mother and father; hence it insists on our first and best loyalty.

"Ask not," said President Kennedy, "what your country can do for *you*, but rather ask what *you* can do for your country." Since the "you" in question is both real and human and the country you are alleged to possess is one of the most extreme of verbal abstractions, it will readily be seen that the president's injunction is an expression of a synthetic family philosophy which regards "nation" as possessing a claim superior to the claim of "family". If you see nothing wrong with this, then it is probable you also believe that, with a little tinkering, our schools will work just fine. But if you have a queer feeling about the image of yourself and your family as appendages of an abstraction, then we are on the same wavelength. In the latter case, we are ready to consider that we may need less school, not more.

III

I want to examine the destructive effects the false claim of institutional prerogative has on both individual and family life, a destructiveness equally profound whether the claim comes from a government, a corporation, or some other form of network.

If we return to our original discussion of networks, it will be clear that every one of our national institutions is a place where men, women, and children are isolated according to some limited aspect of their total humanity: by age, and a few other considerations in the case of compulsory schooling, as well as by various other sorting mechanisms in the other institutional arenas.

If performance within these narrow confines is conceived to be the supreme measure of success, if, for instance, an A average is considered the central purpose of adolescent life — the requirements for which take most of the time and attention of the aspirant — and if the worth of the individual is reckoned by victory or defeat in this abstract pursuit, then a social machine has been constructed which, by attaching purpose and meaning to essentially meaningless and fantastic behavior, will certainly dehumanize students, alienate them from their own human nature, and break the natural connection between them and their parents, to whom they would otherwise look for significant affirmations.

Welcome to the world of mass schooling, which sets this goal as its supreme achievement. Are you sure we want more of it?

As we approach the twenty-first century it is correct to say that the United States has become a nation of institutions, whereas it used to be a nation of communities. Large cities have great difficulty supporting healthy community life, partly because of the coming and going of strangers, partly because of space constrictions, partly because of poisoned environments, but mostly because of the constant competition of institutions and networks

for the custody of children and old people, for monopolizing the time of everyone else in between. By isolating
young and old from the working life of places and by isolating the working population from the lives of young
and old, institutions and networks have brought about a
fundamental disconnection of the generations. The
griefs that arise from this have no synthetic remedy; no
vibrant, satisfying communities can come into being
where young and old are locked away.

Here and there mutilated versions of community
struggle to survive, as in places where cultural homogeneity has been fiercely protected — such as in
Bensonhurst in Brooklyn or Polish Hill in Pittsburgh —
but in the main, "community" in cities and suburbs is a
thin illusion, confined to simulated events like street festivals. If you have moved from one neighborhood to
another or from one suburb to another and have quickly forgotten the friends you left behind, then you will
have experienced the phenomenon I refer to. Over ninety percent of the United States' population now lives
inside fifty urban aggregations. Having been concentrated there as the end product of fairly well-understood
historical processes, they are denied a reciprocal part in
any continuous, well-articulated community. They are
profoundly alienated from their own human interests.
What else could it mean that only half of our eligible citizens are registered to vote? And that of those a barely
fifty percent do vote? In two-party jurisdictions a trifle
over one-eighth of the citizenry is thus sufficient to elect
public officials, assuming the vote splits fairly evenly.
We've come a long way down the road to redefining as

an option what used to be regarded as a duty, but that is what alienation from community life quickly accomplishes: indifference to almost everything.

When one is offered institutional simulations of community, a steady diet of networks — involuntary like schools, or "voluntary" like isolated workplaces divorced from human variety — basic human needs are placed in the gravest jeopardy, a danger magnified many times in the case of children. Institutional goals, however sane and well-intentioned, are unable to harmonize deeply with the uniqueness of individual human goals. No matter how good the individuals who manage an institution are, institutions lack a conscience because they measure by accounting methods. Institutions are not the sum total of their personnel, or even of their leadership, but are independent of both and will exist after management has been completely replaced. They are ideas come to life, ideas in whose service all employees are but servomechanisms. The deepest purposes of these gigantic networks are to regulate and to make uniform. Since the logic of family and community is to give scope to variety around a central theme, whenever institutions intervene significantly in personal affairs they cause much damage. By redirecting the focus of our lives from families and communities to institutions and networks, we, in effect, anoint a machine our king.

IV

Nearly a century ago a French sociologist wrote that every institution's unstated first goal is to survive and grow, *not* to undertake the mission it has nominally staked out for itself. Thus the first goal of a government postal service is not to deliver the mail; it is to provide protection for its employees and perhaps a modest status ladder for the more ambitious ones. The first goal of a permanent military organization is not to defend national security but to secure, in perpetuity, a fraction of the national wealth to distribute to its personnel.

It was this philistine potential — that teaching the young *for pay* would inevitably expand into an institution for the protection of teachers, not students — that made Socrates condemn the Sophists so strongly long ago in ancient Greece.

If this view of things troubles you, think of the New York City public school system in which I work, one of the largest business organizations on planet Earth. While the education administered by this abstract parent is ill-regarded by everybody, the institution's right to *compel* its clientele to accept such dubious service is still guaranteed by the police. And forces are gathering to expand its reach still further — in the face of every evidence that it has been a disaster throughout its history.

What gives the atmosphere of remote country towns and other national backwaters a peculiarly heady quality of fundamental difference is not simply a radical change of scenery from city or suburb, but the promise offered of near freedom from institutional intervention in family life. Big Father doesn't watch over such places closely. Where his presence is felt most is still in the schools, which even there grind out their relentless message of anger, envy, competition, and caste-verification in the form of grades and "classes." But a homelife and community exist there as antidotes to the poison.

This business we call "education" — when we mean "schooling" — makes an interesting example of network values in conflict with traditional community values. For one hundred and fifty years institutional education has seen fit to offer as its main purpose the preparation for economic success. Good education = good job, good money, good *things*. This has become the universal national banner, hoisted by Harvards as well as high schools. This prescription makes both parent and student easier to regulate and intimidate as long as the connection goes unchallenged either for its veracity or in its philosophical truth. Interestingly enough, the American Federation of Teachers identifies one of its missions as persuading the business community to hire and promote on the basis of school grades so that the grades = money formula will obtain, just as it was made to obtain for medicine and law after years of political lobbying. So far, the common sense of businesspeople has kept them hiring and promoting the old-fashioned way, using performance and private judgment as the preferred measures, but they may not resist much longer.

The absurdity of defining education as an economic good becomes clear if we ask ourselves what is gained by perceiving education as a way to enhance even further the runaway consumption that threatens the earth, the air, and the water of our planet? Should we continue to teach people that they can buy happiness in the face of a tidal wave of evidence that they cannot? Shall we ignore the evidence that drug addiction, alcoholism, teenage suicide, divorce, and other despairs are pathologies of the prosperous much more than they are of the poor?

On this question of meanings we've hidden from ourselves for so long hangs both an understanding of the illness that is killing us and the cure we are searching for. What, after all this time, is the purpose of mass schooling supposed to be? Reading, writing, and arithmetic can't be the answer, because properly approached those things take less than a hundred hours to transmit — and we have abundant evidence that each is readily self-taught in the right setting and time.

Why, then, are we locking kids up in an involuntary network with strangers for twelve years? Surely not so a few of them can get rich? Even if it worked that way, and I doubt that it does, why wouldn't any sane community look on such an education as positively wrong? It divides and classifies people, demanding that they compulsively compete with each other, and publicly labels the losers by literally de-grading them, identifying them as "low-class" material. And the bottom line for the winners is that they can buy more *stuff*! I don't believe that anyone who thinks about that feels comfortable with such a silly conclusion. I can't help feeling that if we could only answer the question of what it is that we want from these kids we lock up, we would suddenly see where we took a wrong turn. I have enough faith in American imagination and resourcefulness to believe that at that point we'd come up with a better way — in fact, a whole supermarket of better ways.

One thing I do know, though: most of us who've had a taste of loving families, even a little taste, want our kids to be part of one. One other thing I know is that eventually you have to come to be part of a place — part of its hills and streets and waters and people — or you will live a very, very sorry life as an exile forever. Discovering *meaning for yourself* as well as discovering satisfying *purpose for yourself*, is a big part of what education is. How this can be done by locking children away from the world is beyond me.

V

An important difference between communities and institutions is that communities have natural limits; they *stop* growing or they die. There's a good reason for this: in the best communities everyone is a special person who sooner or later impinges on everyone else's consciousness. The effects of this constant attention make all, rich or poor, feel important, because the only way importance is perceived is by having other folks pay attention to you. You can *buy* attention, of course, but it's not the same thing. Pseudo community life, where you live around others without noticing them and where you are constantly being menaced in some way by strangers you find offensive, is exactly the opposite. In pseudo community life you are anonymous for the most part, and you *want* to be because of various dangers other people may present if they notice your existence. Almost the only way you can get attention in a pseudo community is to buy it, because the prevailing atmosphere is one of indifference. A pseudo community is just a different kind of network: its friendships and loyalties are transient; its problems are universally considered to be someone else's problems (someone else who should be *paid* to solve them); its young and old are largely regarded as annoyances; and the most commonly shared dream is to get out to a better place, to "trade up" endlessly.

Unlike true communities, pseudo communities and other comprehensive networks like schools expand indefinitely, just as long as they can get away with it. "More" may not be "better," but "more" is always more profitable for the people who make a living out of networking. That is what is happening today behind the cry to expand schooling even further: a great many people are going to make a great deal of money if growth can be continued.

Unlike the intricate, sometimes unfathomable satisfactions of community and family life, the successes of networks are always measured in mathematical displays of one-upmanship: How many A's? How much weight lost? How many inquiries generated? Competition is the network's lifeblood, and the precision suggested by the numerical ranking of performance is its preferred style.

The quality-competition of businesses (when it actually happens) is generally a good thing for customers; it keeps businesses on their toes, doing their best. The competition inside an institution like a school isn't the same thing at all. What is competed for in a school is the favor of a teacher, and that can be won or lost by too many subjective parameters to count; it is always a little arbitrary and sometimes a lot more pernicious than that. It gives rise to envy, dissatisfaction, and a belief in magic. Teachers, too, must compete for the arbitrarily dispensed favor of administrators, which carries the promise of good or bad classes, good or bad rooms, access to or denial of tools, and other hostages to obedience, deference, and subordination. The culture of schools only coheres in response to a web of material rewards and punishments: A's, F's, bathroom passes, gold stars, "good" classes, access to a photocopy machine. Everything we know about *why* people drive themselves to know things and do their best is contradicted inside these places.

Truth itself is another important dividing line between communities and networks. If you don't keep your word in a community, everyone finds out, and you have a major problem thereafter. But lying for personal advantage is the operational standard in all large institutions; it is considered part of the game in schools. Parents, for the most part, are lied to or told half-truths, as they are usually considered adversaries. At least that's been true in every school I ever worked in. Only the most foolish employees don't have recourse to lying; the penalties for being caught hardly exist — and the rewards for success can be considerable. Whistle-blowing against institutional malpractice is always a good way to get canned or relentlessly persecuted. Whistle-blowers never get promoted in any institution because, having served a public interest once, they may well do it again.

The Cathedral of Rheims is the best evidence I know of what a community can do and what we stand to lose when we don't know the difference between these human miracles and the social machinery we call "networks." Rheims was built without power tools by people working day and night for a hundred years. Everybody worked willingly; nobody was slave labor. No school taught cathedral building as a subject.

What possessed people to work together for a hundred years? Whatever it was looks like something worth educating ourselves about. We know the workers were profoundly united as families and as friends, and as friends they knew what they really wanted in the way of a church. Popes and archbishops had nothing to do with it. Gothic architecture itself was invented out of sheer aspiration — the Gothic cathedral stands like a lighthouse illuminating what is possible in the way of uncoerced human union. It provides a benchmark against which our own lives can be measured.

At Rheims, the serfs and farmers and peasants filled gigantic spaces with the most incredible stained-glass windows in the world, but they never bothered to sign even one of them. No one knows who designed or made them, because our modern form of institutional boasting did not yet exist as a corruption of communitarian feeling. After all these centuries they still announce what being human really means.

VI

Communities are collections of families and friends who find major meaning in extending the family association to a band of honorary brothers and sisters. They are complex relationships of commonality and obligation that generalize to others beyond the perimeter of the homestead.

When the integration of life that comes from being part of a family in a community is unattainable, the only alternative, apart from accepting a life in isolation, is to search for an artificial integration into one of the many expressions of network currently available. But it's a bad trade! Artificial integration within the realm of human association — think of those college dorms or fraternities — appears strong but is actually quite weak; seems close-knit but in reality has only loose bonds; suggests durability but is usually transient. And it is most often badly adjusted to what people need although it masquerades as being exactly what they need.

Welcome to the world of school. We should begin thinking about school reform by stopping these places from functioning like cysts, impenetrable, insular bodies that take our money, our children, and our time and give nothing back. Do we really want *more* of it?

In recent years I've given much thought to the problem of turning the compulsory school network into some kind of emotionally rewarding community, because a move seems to be afoot to do the reverse, to enlarge substantially the bite that schooling takes out of a young person's family time, community time, and private time. Trial balloons are floated about constantly in the press and on TV, meaning that some important groups are preparing to extend the reach of compulsory schooling in the face of its genuinely ghastly record. My Jewish friends would call that "chutzpah", but I take it as an index of just how confident these people are that they can pull it off.

Schools, I hear it argued, would make better sense and be better value as nine-to-five operations or even nine-to-nine ones, working year-round. We're not a farming community anymore, I hear, that we need to give kids time off to tend the crops. This new-world-order schooling would serve dinner, provide evening recreation, offer therapy, medical attention, and a whole range of other services, which would convert the institution into a true synthetic family for children, better than the original one for many poor kids, it is said — and this would level the playing field for the sons and daughters of weak families.

Yet it appears to me as a schoolteacher that schools are already a major cause of weak families and weak communities. They separate parents and children from vital interaction with each other and from true curiosity about each other's lives. Schools stifle family originality by appropriating the critical time needed for any sound idea of family to develop — then they blame the family for its failure to be a family. It's like a malicious person lifting a photograph from the developing chemicals too early, and then pronouncing the photographer incompetent.

A Massachusetts Senator said a while ago that his state had a higher literacy rate before it adopted compulsory schooling than after. It's certainly an idea worth considering: schools reached their maximum efficiency long ago, meaning that "more" for schools will make things worse, instead of better.

VII

Whatever an education is, it should make you a unique individual, not a conformist; it should furnish you with an original spirit with which to tackle the big challenges; it should allow you to find values which will be your road map through life; it should make you spiritually rich, a person who loves whatever you are doing, wherever you are, whomever you are with; it should teach you what is important: how to live and how to die.

What's gotten in the way of education in the United States is a theory of social engineering that says there is *one right way* to proceed with growing up. That's an ancient Egyptian idea symbolized by the pyramid with an eye on top, the one that's on the other side of George Washington on our one-dollar bill. Everyone is a stone defined by its position on the pyramid. This theory has been presented in many different ways, but at bottom it signals the worldview of minds obsessed with the control of other minds, obsessed by dominance and strategies of intervention to maintain that dominance.

It might have worked for the Pharaohs but it certainly hasn't worked very well for us. Indeed, nothing in the historical record provides evidence that any one idea should dominate the developmental time of all the young, and yet aspirants to monopolize this time have never been closer to winning the prize. The humming of the great hive society foreseen by Francis Bacon, and by H.G. Wells in *The Sleeper Awakes,* has never sounded louder than it does to us right now.

The heart of a defense for the cherished American ideals of privacy, variety, and individuality lies in the way we bring up our young. *Children learn what they live.* Put kids in a class and they will live out their lives in an invisible cage, isolated from their chance at community; interrupt kids with bells and horns all the time and they will learn that nothing is important; force them to plead for the natural right to the toilet and they will become liars and toadies; ridicule them and they will retreat from human association; shame them and they will find a hundred ways to get even. The habits taught in large-scale organizations are deadly.

Individuality, family, and community, on the other hand, are, by definition, expressions of singular organization, never of "one-right-way" thinking on a grand scale. Private time is absolutely essential if a private identity is going to develop, and private time is equally essential to the development of a code of private values, without which we aren't really individuals at all. Children and families need some relief from government surveillance and intimidation if original expressions belonging to *them* are to develop. Without these freedom has no meaning.

The lesson of my teaching life is that both the theory and the structure of mass education are fatally flawed; they cannot work to support the democratic logic of our national idea because they are unfaithful to the democratic principle. The democratic principle is still the best idea for a nation, even though we aren't living up to it right now.

Mass education cannot work to produce a fair society because its daily practice is practice in rigged competition, suppression, and intimidation. The schools we've allowed to develop can't work to teach nonmaterial values, the values which give meaning to everyone's life, rich or poor, because the structure of schooling is held together by a Byzantine tapestry of reward and threat, of carrots and sticks. Official favor, grades, or other trinkets of subordination have no connection with education; they are the paraphernalia of servitude, not of freedom.

Mass schooling damages children. We don't need any more of it. And under the guise that it is the same thing as education, it has been picking our pockets just as Socrates predicted it would thousands of years ago. One of the surest ways to recognize real education is by the fact that it doesn't cost very much, doesn't depend on expensive toys or gadgets. The experiences that produce it and the self-awareness that propels it are nearly free. It is hard to turn a dollar on education. But schooling is a wonderful hustle, getting sharper all the time.

Sixty-five years ago Bertrand Russell, one of the great mathematicians of this century, its greatest philosopher, and a close relation of the King of England to boot, saw that mass schooling in the United States had a profoundly anti-democratic intent, that it was a scheme to artificially deliver national unity by eliminating human variation and by eliminating the forge that produces variation: the family. According to Lord Russell, mass schooling produced a recognizably *American* student: anti-intellectual, superstitious, lacking self-confidence, and having less of what Russell called "inner freedom" than his or her counterpart in any other nation he knew of, past or present. These schooled children became citizens, he said, with a thin "mass character," holding excellence and aesthetics equally in contempt, being inadequate to the personal crises of their lives.

American national unity has always been the central problem of American life. It was inherent in our synthetic beginnings and in the conquest of a continental landmass. It was true in 1790 and it is just as true, perhaps even truer, two hundred years later. Somewhere around the time of the Civil War we began to try shortcuts to get the unity we wanted faster, by artificial means. Compulsory schooling was one of those shortcuts, perhaps the most important one. "Take hold the children!" said John Cotton back in colonial Boston, and that seemed such a good idea that eventually the people who looked at "unity" almost as if it were a religious idea did just that. It took thirty years to beat down a fierce opposition, but by the 1880s it had come to pass — "they" had the children. For the last one hundred and ten years, the "one-right-way" crowd has been trying to figure out what to do with the children, and they still don't know.

Perhaps it is time to try something different. "Good fences make good neighbors," said Robert Frost. The natural solution to learning to live together in a community is first to learn to live apart as individuals and as families. Only when you feel good about yourself can you feel good about others.

But we attacked the problem of unity mechanically, as though we could force an engineering solution by crowding the various families and communities under the broad, homogenizing umbrella of institutions like compulsory schools. The outcome of this scheme was that the democratic ideas that were the only justification for our national experiment were betrayed.

The attempt at a shortcut continues, and it ruins families and communities now, just as it did then. Rebuild these things and young people will begin to educate themselves with our help — just as they did at the nation's beginning. They don't have anything to work for now except money, and that's never been a first-class motivator. Break up these institutional schools, decertify teaching, let anyone who has a mind to teach bid for customers, privatize this whole business — trust the free market system. I know it's easier said than done, but what other choice do we have? We need less school, not more.

Chapter

5

THE CONGREGATIONAL PRINCIPLE

THE BEGINNING OF AN AMERICAN SOLUTION TO OUR SCHOOL PROBLEM

This talk, eventually one of the most popular arrows in my peripatetic speaker's quiver, began life in a slightly altered form as an essay in The Maine Scholar.

T HESE ARE SURREALISTIC TIMES. The scientific school establishment continues to float plans for further centralization in the form of national standards, a national curriculum, and improved national standardized testing. Magical promises are everywhere: machines are the answer; massive interventions are the answer; new forms of pre-schooling are the answer; baseball bats, bullhorns, and padlocks are the answer. In the face of a century and a half of searching for it unsuccessfully, nobody seems to doubt for a minute that there is an answer. One answer. The one right answer.

Perhaps you agree, perhaps not. But if some lingering doubt exists in your mind about the possibility of a central prescription ever touching the school disease, then come with me for a while back to Colonial New England where a different theory of institutions existed, a theory which might lead to the best kind of rethinking/reform, where serious mistakes are self-limiting and, in historical terms, quickly foreclosed by natural market mechanisms. Come with me to the coasts of Colonial New England, to towns like Salem and Marblehead, Framingham and Dedham, Wellfleet and Provincetown. Consider a different perspective that grew out of the soil of a New World, a perspective that shocked other nations with the productivity of its genius.

This new system began with the first Puritan church at Salem, organized in 1629 by the so-called "Salem Procedure." No "higher-up" was around to approve the selection of the church authorities, so the congregation took that responsibility upon themselves. With that simple act, they took power that had traditionally belonged to some certified expert and placed it in the hands of people who went to church. That was the sole criterion of governance: that a voter took going to church seriously and joined a congregation as evidence. It was an act of monumental localism. For the next two hundred years that simple shedding of traditional authority corroded the monopoly power of the state and church to broadcast uniform versions of the truth. Each separate congregation took a vigorous role in particularizing its own parish through debate of lay members, not through the centralization inherent in pronouncement by outside authority. Each separate congregation took on responsibility for solving its own problems —

whether of education, economics, or doctrine — rather than submitting to the old authority of England or to the new aristocracy of expertise.

❖   ❖   ❖

Last fall I spoke in the town of Dedham at a church built in 1638, only nine years after the *Arbella* brought the Nonconformists to Boston. The church I spoke in was Unitarian Universalist, but had originally been Congregational. White spire, strikingly plain, graceful lines — the simplicity and rightness of Congregational church architecture is absolutely unmistakable, remarkable, and uniform. You may or may not be aware that the style of worship that went with this style of architecture was the original and exclusive religion of the Massachusetts Bay Colony, from the Salem Procedure until 1834, over two hundred years of what seems on the surface to be a "one-right-way" religion. You were either a Congregationalist or you weren't anything you dared speak of in public, at least without risk of being shunned, persecuted, or even burned at the stake. So far this sounds even worse than the school monopoly that ruins us, doesn't it?

These Congregationalists were so jealously protective of their monopoly that one hundred and seventy years ago, when Lyman Beecher got word that Unitarians were on their way out from the bowels of hell, he rode through the streets just like Paul Revere warning, "The Unitarians are coming! The Unitarians are coming!" You'll gather Parson Beecher wasn't exactly thrilled with their advent. But an amazing thing happened over the next century. The Congregationalists slowly changed their minds *without being forced to do so.* By the end of the 1800s, the Unitarians were well-respected throughout New England.

Most people think of Colonial New England as embodying the greatest period of conformity this country has ever seen. But the nature of Congregationalism hides a very great irony: structurally, this way of life demands individuality, not regimentation. The service is almost free of liturgy, emphasizing local preaching about local issues. This virtually guarantees *dissonance* inside the congregation. The constant struggle for clarity by every church member acting as his or her own priest, his or her own expert, invariably leads to progress toward truth. Why do I say that? Well, what I've just described is the process that Aristotle and Karl Marx and Thomas Hobbes and any of a large number of creative thinkers have called "the dialectic." The Congregational procedure was dialectical down to its roots, in a way acutely hostile to hierarchical thinking.

Central planners of any period despise the dialectic because it gets in the way of efficiently broadcasting "one right way" to do things. Half a century ago Bertrand Russell remarked that the United States was the only major country on earth that deliberately avoided teaching its children to think dialectically. He was talking about twentieth-century America, of course, the land of compulsory government schooling, not the New England of Congregational distinction. Did you wonder where "Yankees" got their lasting reputation for stubbornness, orneriness, and shrewd hair-splitting? Now you know. Roger Williams saw as clearly as any person of his time and recognized the inevitable connection between dissonance and quality of life. You can't have one without the other.

Much recent scholarship has shown the towns of Massachusetts in the seventeenth century not to be uniform at all, but to be laboratories of local choice and style. Each had considerable flexibility to deviate from what might have been central governmental rule. The town of Dedham, where I spoke last fall, drew its original settlers from East Anglia in England, a place that favored private ownership and individual choice. The institutions of East Anglia quickly established themselves in the New World too. On the other hand, Sudbury, the town next to Dedham, had been populated by colonists of Saxon and Celtic background, who traditionally shared their work. Just as they had done in Britain they held open fields in common in America. In Colonial Massachusetts, then, there was creative tension between the common culture of the region and the local village culture. Like tension in music or poetry between a regular pattern and creative departures from it, this tension among the small towns and among the different congregations and inside each separate congregation produced an astonishing energy, a fertile and idiosyncratic peculiarity that characterized the particular genius that distinguished colonial Massachusetts.

Now I want us to examine something that seems embarrassing in New England civil life; and yet, paradoxically, I think it hides a secret of great power, which the social engineers who built and maintain our government monopoly schools are forced to overlook: *Each town was able to exclude people it didn't like*! People were able to *choose* whom they wanted to work with, to sort themselves into a living curriculum that worked for them. The words of the first Dedham charter catch this feeling perfectly; the original settlers wanted to (and did) shut out "people whose dispositions do not suit us, whose society will be hurtful to us." So in a funny way these early towns functioned like selective *clubs* or colleges, like MIT and Harvard do today, narrowing human differences down to a range that could be managed by them humanely. If you consider the tremendous stresses the dialectical process sets up anyway — where all people are their own priests, their own final masters — it's hard to see how a congregational society can do otherwise. If you have to accept everyone, no matter how hostile they may be to your own personality, philosophy, or mission, then an operation would quickly become paralyzed by fatal disagreements. The common causes and purposes that mark human association at its best would then degrade into those few innocuous undertakings that have no political dimension, if such can be found.

It's a subtle distinction: living dialectically as the New Englanders did produces spectacular accomplishments and brings out strong qualities of character and mind in individuals, but it isn't possible to manage where the whole catalogue of human beings is thrown together haphazardly or forced together, as it is in government monopoly school life. To prevent chaos in these places, management must aim, by hook or by crook, to make everything — time, space, texts, and procedures — as uniform as possible. The Greeks had a story about a man who did just that; his name was Procustes. He cut or stretched travelers to fit his guest bed. The system worked perfectly, but it played havoc with the traveler.

These New Englanders invented a system where people who wanted to live and work together could do so. Yet the whole region seemed to prosper in wonderful ways: materially, intellectually, and socially. It was almost as if by taking care of your own business you succeeded in some magical fashion in taking care of pubic business too. The habits of self-reliance, self-respect, fearlessness, democracy, and local loyalty produced good citizens. Government monopoly schools use a different blueprint these days, of course. People are drawn willy-nilly out of large "catchment" areas and dumped together into compartments according to similar scores on standardized tests. There they are exhorted to perform and behave according to the specifications of strangers. Christopher Lasch writes in *The True and Only Heaven:*

> The capacity for loyalty is stretched too thin when it tries to attach itself to the hypothetical solidarity of the human race. It needs to attach itself to specific people and specific places, not to an abstract ideal of universal human rights. We love particular men and women, not humanity in general.

This catches a piece of what's wrong with compulsory schools as large as New England towns, schools that don't allow any choice of curricula, philosophy, or companions. Wendell Berry catches another piece of it in a letter to a magazine editor:

I don't think "global thinking" is futile, I think it is impossible. You can't think about what you don't know and nobody knows this planet. Some people know a little about a few small parts of it ... The people who think globally do so by abstractly and statistically reducing the globe to quantities. Political tyrants and industrial exploiters have done this most successfully. Their concepts and their greed are abstract and their abstractions lead with terrifying directness and simplicity to acts that are invariably destructive. If you want to do good and preserving acts you must think and act locally. The effort to do good acts gives the global game away. You can't do a good act that is global ... a good act, to be good, must be acceptable to what Alexander Pope called "the genius of the place." This calls for local knowledge, local skills, and local love that virtually none of us has, and that none of us can get by thinking globally. We can get it only by a local fidelity that we would have to maintain through several lifetimes ... I don't wish to be loved by people who don't know me; if I were a planet I would feel exactly the same way.

Local skills, local knowledge, local love, and local fidelity were what the forge of Congregationalism in New England produced best, but there was a negative side to this localism as well.

The religious discrimination of early New England was a way of ensuring enough local harmony that a community of people who suited each other could arise bearing a common vision. Here is a scene from three hundred years ago in the town of Dedham, Massachusetts, which could have been witnessed from the very church where I spoke: three Quaker women are stripped to the waist and whipped the length of town, tied to the tail of a cart. It would be an understatement to say that such treatment underlined the fact that the Quaker disposition was not one of those suited to Dedham. But then, for that matter, neither was the Presbyterian disposition. John Milton himself had written that the "new Presbyter is but old Priest writ large," and so all Presbyterians were driven off to the wilds of New Jersey where they founded Princeton. Of course, it was equally bad for your health to be a Catholic in Dedham, or to be a Leveller, a Digger, or a Hutterite. In this detestable fashion Dedham was able to enjoy 234 years of religious purity before its Congregational monopoly was broken.

Well, what does this all mean? Just this: the negative side of local choice is very easy to see and even very easy to predict. We see it illustrated in the example of Colonial Dedham. But the whole matter is a good deal more complicated than assigning a bad grade to religious discrimination or to any other type of social choice that prescribes and limits a particular kind of human association. For instance, where could we begin to look for an explanation of how these people grew gradually more tolerant and came to accept all forms of religion? They even changed their conservative ways to the point where Massachusetts gained a national reputation as the most liberal state in the Union. That's quite a flip-flop to account for in the absence of compulsion, intimidation, or potent enabling legislation, isn't it. How did Dedham and the rest of those towns *teach themselves* to reform without experts making them do it and without central intervention? Remember, they only allowed the practitioners of one religion to vote. But they changed! And nobody forced them to do it! Something mysterious inside the structure of Congregationalism worked to have them abandon some of the exclusivity that adherence to Biblical elite dogma had taught them.

I am certain that "something" was nearly unconditional local choice. And it was self-correcting! Because the town churches did not team up to present an institutional orthodoxy that made each town just like another — as government monopoly schools do today — error in one church could be countered by its correction in another. As long as people had the choice to vote with their feet, the free market punished severe errors by leaving a congregation empty, just as it could reward a good place by filling it up. And even if enough rotten people were found to make a rotten town or rotten congregation, as long as there was no machinery in place for that one idea to compel all others to bow down before it, the human damage it could cause was strictly limited. Only when situations exist out of which a central orthodoxy can arise, like a pyramid, is there a real danger that some central poison can poison us all.

❖   ❖   ❖

Yes, the negative aspects of local choice are easy to spot, and the overwhelming argument in its favor — that without it the genius of democracy cannot exist — is hard to see. Because there is plenty of local tyranny as well, the temptation is to cede power to a central authority in the name of fairness, to manage some best way for all from central headquarters. That's what a national curriculum is supposed to be for schools, a rational, fair way to legislate bad schooling out of existence. A national curriculum would never have allowed Dedham or Sudbury or Framingham or Wellfleet to develop as they did; that would have been dangerous, unpredictable, divisive — no, they would have been regulated centrally, as our schools are today, even without a national curriculum and national standards.

And here comes the dialectic. The experience of our centrally planned century has not been very good for most people. According to some, the planet itself is in jeopardy. And things legislated out of existence, like alcohol and drug abuse or racism, don't seem to go away as religious exclusivity went away naturally in New England under a regime of local choice; instead, law appears to give bad habits an injection of virulent new life. Think of the great progressive victories won in the courts because social engineers were unable to build popular consensus, or were unwilling to wait: affirmative action, desegregation, restrictions on graphic sexual imagery available at the local newsstand, various women's rights issues, and so on. Are these victories for the groups the courts sought to protect, or do these victories hold the same value they would have, had they been won through change in the social consensus? By most parameters the plight of Black Americans, for example, now seems to be worse than it was in 1960. Furthermore, a mean-spiritedness seems to exist everywhere, including in our schools, that pours contempt and neglect on further efforts to give the descendants of slavery a hand. The predicament of women is a little trickier to see, but if sharply accelerated rates of suicide, heart disease, emotional illness, sterility, and other pathological conditions are an indicator, the admission of women *en masse* to the unisex workplace is not an unmixed blessing. Further, some disturbing evidence exists that the income of working *couples* in 1990 has only slightly more purchasing power than the income of the average working man did in 1910. In effect, two laborers are now being purchased for the price of one — an outcome Adam Smith or David Ricardo might have predicted. And an unseen social cost of all of this has been the destruction of family life, the loss of home as sanctuary or haven, and the bewilderment of children who, since infancy, have been raised by strangers.

Does central legal intimidation produce the social results it promises? Not so long ago narcotics were legal in the United States; while they were always a pernicious nuisance, they never became an epidemic before legislation prohibiting their use came into existence. Is it possible that *compelling* people to do something guarantees that they will do it poorly, with a bad will, or indifferently, unless you are willing, as the Army is, to suspend most human rights and use any degree of intimidation necessary? And if the latter is the only way that compulsion can produce results, what is the *human* value of using it if it diminishes the quality of human life?

Multiple prohibitions of choice in the matter of education are now enforced by law, enshrining an exclusive bureaucracy of certified teachers and administrators, and literally hundreds of invisible agencies necessary to maintain the institution of government monopoly schooling. Defying the lessons of the market, this psychopathic megalith has grown more and more powerful in spite of colossal failures to educate throughout its history. It succeeds in surviving only because it employs the police power of the State to fill its hollow classrooms. It prohibits local choice and variety and, because of this prohibition, has had a hideous effect on our national moral fabric. The effect the national prohibition of alcohol by legislation has had on social cohesion and common values is an object lesson too recent to forget, I hope. And compared to the prohibitions that compulsory government monopoly schooling imposes on the children and families of a nation, alcohol prohibition is a minor episode. By preventing a free market in education, a handful of social engineers, backed by the industries that profit from compulsory schooling — teacher colleges, textbook publishers, materials suppliers, and others — has ensured that most of our children will not have an education, even though they may be thoroughly schooled.

Divorced from religion, the congregational principle is a psychological force propelling individuals to reach their maximum potential when working in small groups of people with whom they feel in harmony. If you think about this you wonder what purpose is achieved by arranging things any other way. The Congregationalists understood profoundly that good things happen to the human spirit *when it is left alone.*

The best immediate evidence I have to offer, that leaving people alone to work out their own local destinies is a splendid idea, is the curious sociology of my presence as a speaker in Dedham last year. There, in a community that had whipped half-naked Quaker women, stood I — a Roman Catholic with a Scots Presbyterian wife, accompanied by my good friend Roland, half pagan, half Jewish — in a Unitarian Universalist church that had once been Congregational. No act of the Massachusetts legislature made that possible, no pronouncement of the Supreme Court. People learned to be neighbors in Dedham because for three hundred years they were allowed real choice, including the choice to make their own mistakes. Everyone learned a better way to deal with difference than exclusion because they had time to think about it and to work it through — time measured in generations.

But if they had been *ordered* to change, ordered, as other immigrants were, to change their behavior and to abandon their culture in compulsory schools set up for that purpose, I think what would have happened is this: some of them would have *seemed* to change but would have harbored such powerful resentments at being deprived of choice that some way to exact vengeance would have evolved. And most of the group deprived of choice and custom and family and roots would have reacted in a variety of ways to these social pressures, would have gone quietly insane or become simplified people, fit to haul stones to build someone else's pyramids, perhaps, or to watch television's simplified fantasies, but fit for little else.

Despite the lip service we have continued to pay to local choice ever since Congregational days, our schools are centrally planned and already have a national curricu-

lum in place mediated by the textbook publishing industry and the standardized training of teachers. That our
schools have failed spectacularly to give our children the
education we want for them, or the selves we want, or to
deliver on the dream of the democratic, classless society
we still yearn for is obvious enough; what we miss is the
logic of our failure. By allowing the imposition of direction from centers far beyond our control, we have time
and again missed the lesson of the Congregational principle: *people are less than whole unless they gather themselves
voluntarily* into groups of souls in harmony. Gathering
themselves to pursue individual, family, and community
dreams consistent with their private humanity is what
makes them whole; only slaves are gathered by others.
And these dreams must be written locally because to
exercise any larger ambition without such a base is to lose
touch with the things which give life meaning: self, family, friends, work, and intimate community.

❖   ❖   ❖

There seem to me to be two "official" ways to look at the
state of education in the United States these days, both
of them wrong. First, we conceive it to be an engineering problem that can be made to yield to a pragmatic
instrumental approach. From this vantage point there is
a simple right and wrong way of schooling, never the
thousand private individual possibilities the New
England Congregationalists might have believed in.
Second, we look upon schooling as if it were a character
in a continuous courtroom drama, a drama wherein we
search for the villains who have prevented our kids from

learning. Bad teachers, poor textbooks, incompetent administrators, evil politicians, ill-trained parents, bad children — whoever the villains may be we shall find them, indict them, arraign them, prosecute them, perhaps even execute them! Then things will be okay.

Out of these two wrong-headed ways of looking at education have grown enormous industries that claim power to cure mass education of its frictions or of its demons in exchange for treasure. Into this carnival of magical thinking has come a parade of profit-seekers: analysts, consultants, researchers, academic houses, writers, advisors, columnists, textbook committees, school boards, testing corporations, journalists, teachers' colleges, state departments of education, monitors, coordinators, manufacturers, certified teachers and administrators, television programs, and hordes of school-related businesses — all parasitic growths of the government monopoly over the school concept.

To many of us, the greatest attraction of social engineering and antisocial demonologies is that both, at bottom, promise a quick fix. That has always been the dark side of the American dream, the search for an easy way out, a belief in magic. The endless parade of promises that constitutes the heart of American advertising, one of the largest of our national enterprises, testifies to the deep well of superstition in our national foundation, which has been institutionalized in the advertising business. Easy money, easy health, easy beauty, easy education — if only the right incantation can be found. Lurking behind the magic is an image of people as machinery that can be built and repaired. This is our

Calvinist legacy calling to us over the centuries, saying that the world and all its living variety is just machinery, not very hard to adjust if we put sentimentality aside and fire the villains, either symbolically or with actual bonfires, depending on the century. School reform to most of us is an engineer reaching for the right wrench or Perry Mason finding the clue he needs to nail the bad guy.

❖ ❖ ❖

Ultimately, how we think about social problems depends on our philosophy of human nature: what we think people are, what we think they are capable of, what the purposes of human existence may be, if any. If people are machines, then school can only be a way to make these machines more reliable; the logic of machines dictates that parts be uniform and interchangeable, all operations time-constrained, predictable, economical. Does this sound to you like the schools you attended, that your children attend? The Civil War unfortunately demonstrated beyond the shadow of a doubt both the financial and social utility of regimentation, but while this notion of people as machines has been around for thousands of years, its effective reign has only been operational since the end of World War I.

American education teaches by its methodology that people are machines. Bells ring, circuits open and close, energy flows or is constricted, qualities are reduced to a numbering system, a plan is followed of which the machine parts know nothing. Octavio Paz from Mexico, the 1990 winner of the Nobel Prize for Literature, has this to say about our schools:

> In the North American system men and women are
> subjected from childhood to an inexorable process.
> Certain principles contained in brief formulas are
> endlessly repeated by the press, radio, television,
> churches, and especially schools. A person impris-
> oned by these schemes is like a plant in a flowerpot
> too small for it. He cannot grow or mature. This sort
> of conspiracy cannot help but provoke violent indi-
> vidual rebellions.

We cannot grow or mature, like plants in too little
flowerpots. We are addicted to dependency; in the current
national crisis of maturity we seem to be waiting for the
teacher to tell us what to do, but the teacher never comes
to do that. Bridges collapse, men and women sleep on the
streets, bankers cheat, good will decays, families betray each
other, the government lies as a matter of policy — corruption, shame, sickness, and sensationalism are everywhere.
No school has a curriculum to provide the quick fix.

The old Congregationalists would have been able to
put their finger at once on the reason pyramidal societies,
such as the one our monopoly form of schooling sustains,
must always end in apathy and disorganization. At the root
they are based on the lie that there is "one right way" in
human affairs and that experts can be awarded the permanent direction of the enterprise of education. It is a lie
because the changing dynamics of time and situation and
locality render expertise irrelevant and obsolete shortly
after it is anointed.

Monopoly schooling has been the chief training
institution of the hive society. It certifies permanent
experts who enjoy privileges of status unwarranted by
the results they produce. Because these privileges, once

achieved, will not willingly be given over, whole appara-
tuses of privilege have been fashioned that are
impregnable to change. Even under the severest criti-
cism they grow larger and more dangerous because they
nourish important parts of our political and economic
system. In the most literal sense they are impossible to
reform because they have ceased to be human, having
been transformed into abstract structures of superb efficiency, independent of lasting human control survival
mechanisms. This is not a devil you can wrestle with as
Daniel Webster did with Old Scratch, but one that has
to be starved to death by depriving it of victims.

Monopoly schooling is the major cause of our loss
of national and individual identity. Having institutionalized the division of social classes and acted as an agent
of caste, it is repugnant to our founding myths and to
the reality of our founding period. Its strength arises
from many quarters, the antichild, antifamily stream of
history being one — but it draws it greatest power from
being a natural adjunct to the kind of commercial economy we have that requires permanently dissatisfied
consumers.

❖   ❖   ❖

It's time to stop. This system doesn't work, and it's one
of the causes of our world coming apart. No amount of
tinkering will make the school machine work to produce
educated people; *education and schooling are, as we all
have experienced, mutually exclusive terms.* In 1930, sixty
long years ago, Thomas Briggs, delivering the Inglis
Lecture at Harvard, charged that "the nation's great

investment in secondary education has shown no respectable achievement"; two decades later, in 1951, a survey made of 30,000 Los Angeles school children discovered that seventy-five percent of eighth graders couldn't find the Atlantic Ocean on a map and most of them couldn't calculate fifty percent of thirty-six. From my personal experience, I stand witness that the situation is certainly no better today.

What on earth is going on? Any genuine debate would have to grapple with the uniform failure of every type of government monopoly school. With the addition of television, the destructive power of schooling is now awesome and thoroughly out of control. The television institution, very similar to the structure of mass schooling, has expanded so successfully that all the former escape routes are now blocked. We have destroyed the minds and characters of the nation's children by preempting their youth, removing their choices. We will pay a huge price in lost humanity for this crime for another century, even if a way is found to overturn the pyramid. Getting rid of the monopoly is the beginning of an answer.

What is there to do? Look to Dedham, to Sudbury, to Marblehead, and to Provincetown, all different yet all capable of meeting their community's needs. Turn your back on national solutions and toward communities of families as successful laboratories. Let us turn inward until we master the first directive of any philosophy worthy of the name: "Know Thyself." Understand that successful communities know the truth of the maxim "Good fences make good neighbors," while at the same time being able to recognize, respect, understand, appreciate, and learn from each other's differences.

Look to the Congregational principle for answers. Encourage and underwrite experimentation; trust children and families to know what's best for themselves; stop the segregation of children and the aged in walled compounds; involve everyone in every community in the education of the young: businesses, institutions, old people, whole families; look for local solutions and always accept a personal solution in place of a corporate one. You need not fear educational consequences: reading, writing, and arithmetic aren't very hard to teach if you take pains to see that compulsion and the school agenda don't short-circuit each individual's private appointment with themselves to learn these things. There is abundant evidence that less than a hundred hours is sufficient for a person to become totally literate and a self-teacher. Don't be panicked by scare tactics into surrendering your children to experts.

Teaching must, I think, be decertified as quickly as possible. That certified teaching experts like me are deemed necessary to make learning happen is a fraud and a scam. Look around you: the results of teacher-college licensing are in the schools you see. Let anybody teach who wants to; give families back their tax money to pick and choose — who could possibly be a better shopper if the means for comparison were made available? Restore the Congregational system by encouraging competition after a truly unmanipulated free-market model — in that way the social dialectic can come back to life. Trust in families and neighborhoods and individuals to make sense of the important question, "What is education for?" If some of them answer differently from what you might prefer, that's really not your business, and it shouldn't be your problem. Our type of schooling has deliberately concealed the fact that such a question must be framed and not taken for granted if anything beyond a mockery of democracy is to be nurtured. It is illegitimate to have an expert answer that question for you. It was our own trust in our own potential that helped lay down good foundations back in the colonial period. I feel certain that the structure we built then still houses powerful potential. Let's use it once again, and create a truly American solution to the great school nightmare.

Afterword

To the Tenth Anniversary Edition

GREETINGS! As I sit here trying to think of something to say that might illuminate the effect *Dumbing Us Down* continues to have on my life and the lives of others, faxes, letters, e-mails, notes, and manuscripts have completely taken over my six-room apartment in Manhattan as well as my 128-acre farm in upstate New York, each and every one bearing on some aspect of the institutional soup I began to stir with the publication of that book.

My correspondents honor me with words I hardly deserve: "Thank you for your dedication to the task of unraveling this pestilence. Tears come to my eyes from an odd mix of joy and anger." A former teacher had this to say: "This book tied together many loose ends that I felt intuitively but could not pin down. I bought twelve copies, sharing them with co-workers and many friends. Because of your book, one of these families has made the decision to homeschool while several others are now contemplating doing so." Over the years I've had nearly a thousand letters like that, from all over the world, tying the decision to homeschool to a chance encounter with *Dumbing Us Down*. From Cuajimalpa, Mexico, came this one: "I had refused my wife's idea to homeschool our children until I read your book. What an impact it made in my life! Now I'm happy to see the rapid development of my daughters in the loving environment of our home."

So is it false modesty that forces me to say that I hardly deserve such praise? Not so, for only I can be aware of how little I had to do, consciously, with the writing of this book; more honestly it should be seen as a book that wrote itself, using me as scribe and confessor.

Over the decade since *Dumbing Us Down* first saw the light of day, a full fifteen thousand of its readers took pains to see that I knew their personal reactions to the book's ideas and to augment my insights into the dismal reality of forced schooling with their own. A dazzling, exhausting, humbling, exhilarating torrent of protest — an outrage distilled from years of confinement, limitation, and humiliation, years of intimidation, of chasing prizes not worth winning, of lost opportunities, of ruined relationships, often with one's own parents, family, neighbors, friends, and self, that came, at times, close to drowning me in grief.

I could answer only a fraction of these communications, yet their cumulative presence and continual arrival, year after year, makes me conscious of just how widespread the harm institutional schooling inflicts really is — and of how grimly aware its victims are of the things it has caused them to lose, the greatest of which is self-knowledge, along with, perhaps, the capacity to fully love. *Dumbing Us Down* has been the catalyst that floats buried memories to the surface: it reminds thousands of men and women of the moments when they struggled to be themselves, only to be broken to a meaner destiny by bells, insults, and standardized tests. The otherwise silent majority wrote to me because they wanted at least one other person to know how they had been wronged.

How did I come to write *Dumbing Us Down?* When I won the first of my Teacher of the Year awards in 1990, I intended to do nothing at the ceremony except to thank the presenter and to wave at my daughter in the audience or, if I were bold enough, to ask her to the podium for a public hug (I was; I did). But on the evening before the ceremony, a student from many years past called to offer congratulations. He casually asked what I intended by way of remarks.

Remarks? I set him straight, or so I thought. "Nobody," I told him, "wants to hear a public school teacher make a speech." There would be no remarks.

"But you *have* to make speech," he demanded. "You have to speak for me, for Wendy, for Amy, for Bruce, for Tamir, for Janet, Jane, Jill, Andy; for all your classes over the years you have to sum up what it's all meant."

"No one will listen," I said.

"I'll listen," he said.

And so that's how "The Psychopathic School" came to be written, in one blaze of all-night coffee-drenched passion. As I expected, the officials of the school district (which actively disliked me) presenting me with the plaque in a Harlem school the next evening neither listened nor commented on my words. But over the next six months I received hundreds of requests to reprint the text. A chunk of it was even entered into the Congressional Record by Senator Bob Kerrey of Nebraska.

"The Psychopathic School," the key essay in this book, deals with a number of pathological patterns I had noticed in schoolchildren over the years, in rich kids as well as in poor. My speech's rapid dissemination all over the land, by word of mouth and small journal, quickly led to requests for an explanation of what specific mechanisms might account for these pathologies.

It was a worthy challenge that took eighteen months of wrestling with myself to answer. Just in time for the ceremony in Albany naming me New York State Teacher of the Year for 1991, I began to see clearly my own role in the crime. Thus parts of "The Seven-Lesson Schoolteacher" comprise my acceptance speech before the state commissioner of education — and soon, that one, too, was reprinted in hundreds of journals, op-ed pages, and homeschool magazines. Both of these talks were finished at the last minute, cost me a groaning to write, and did not arise from any process of ratiocination that I had been familiar with. They "emerged" from my fingertips in the wee hours of the morning, surprising me as much as they did my audience.

Giving these speeches (and there were others, each a chapter in this book) led directly to another phenomenon, which challenged some of my most dearly-held assumptions: there was an outpouring of invitations to speak to groups so diverse that, had they been assembled together in one room, they surely would have killed one another! Suffice it to say that in short order a fellow from Monongahela, Pennsylvania, who had spent most of his adult life speaking to 13-year-old children found himself speaking in the western

White House, in the Old Senate Office Building, to the Cato Institute, the Nashville Center for the Arts, the NASA Space Center's "Engineers' Colloquium", Apple Computers, the Eagle Forum, the United Technologies Corporation, and the Farm Commune as well as before government bureaus in Singapore, Kuala Lumpur, Bogota, and elsewhere — enough places to account for one and a half million miles of travel in the past ten years.

Although I altered the rhetorical clothing to fit the various audiences and situations, my core message was (and remains) that forced institutional schooling is absolutely unreformable because it is already an unqualified success! It does brilliantly precisely what it was originally designed to do, that is, to be the "educational" component of a centralized mass production economy directed from a handful of command centers. Such an economy has desperate needs: in order to work, it requires a particular kind of "human resource," specifically one driven to define itself by purchasing things, by owning "stuff," by evaluating everything from the perspective of comfort, physical security, and status.

Schools are a great mechanism to condition the onrushing generations to accept total management, to impose a kind of lifelong childishness on most of us in the interests of scientific management. Efficient management requires incomplete people to manage because whole people, or those who aspire to wholeness, reject extended tutelage. It's impossible to grow up under total management, whether that's total *quality* management or any other version. Centralized mass production economies, however, can demand no less than this if they are to survive.

The piece "Green Monongahela," like the others, was written in response to my auditors' constant questions about who I was and how I'd come to think this way. It has a hidden agenda that I'm now prepared to expose: I wanted to show all the people who bore scars from their upbringing (that experts of various stripes spin theories of lifelong limitation about), that social "science" is mostly hooey — and dangerous hooey at that. It exists to justify pseudo-scientifically the multiple subordinations which modern management imposes on the managed. If I could demonstrate through my own example that I turned out okay, even though I sprang from a family of eccentric geniuses who fought one another tooth and nail on a daily basis; that I became independent, self-reliant, civil, and reasonably principled even though, had the authorities known some of the events which transpired behind our doors, we would have been in deep trouble, I might become a mirror in which others could see their own stories reflected. And affirmed. By my own example I hoped to become a living refutation to the cult of anointed expertise which has poisoned every aspect of our liberties. Time we were done with this thing. This was once a land where every sane person knew how to build a shelter, grow food, and entertain one another. Now we have been rendered permanent children. It's the architects of forced schooling who are responsible for that.

I credit any success I had in finding a way to be valuable to young people to the accident of my family and the accident of growing up in a place —

Monongahela — where people punched anyone who minded their business too closely. And to the fact that my libertarian upbringing turned me, inadvertently, into a saboteur of oppressive schemes. Lest that pass as idle hyperbole, let me confess that every single day of my life as a schoolteacher I chanted a litany to myself while shaving in the morning. In it I pledged to find, that very day, a way, however small, to throw sand in the gears of the system. Someday I'll write about the particulars, but probably under a *nom de plume* because the details would surely result in a stretch behind bars! I urge all of you who ask me about what to do in your own schools to become such saboteurs, to become little drops of water that erode this waste land of forced institutional schooling.

The last two essays in the book, "We Need Less School, Not More" and "The Congregational Principle," represent my attempts to find the broad outlines of a solution to the problem of modern schooling. Once, long ago, we had the problem solved and became a beacon of hope to others because of it. The rise of industrial society — with cheap, unlimited energy promising riches without precedent, if only the liberty impulses of ordinary people could be reined in — covered the traces of those earlier discoveries, yet not so deeply that they can't be unearthed again, that they can't be resurrected and become the banner to follow. Read these essays slowly, forgetting how comprehensively schooling destroyed your grasp of the vital nature of historical understanding, argue with the nuances of my reasoning — the best America is about argument, not about premature consensus. Both pieces explore inexpensive alternatives to the inane institution that chokes the life out of our children.

Since *Dumbing Us Down*, I've written four other books, one an epic poem, still unpublished, called "The Adventures of Snider, the CIA Spider." But *Dumbing Us Down* remains my favorite because it opened my eyes to the harm I had caused in order to make a living.

These days I'm trying to build a rural retreat and library on 128 acres I own in upstate New York. I want to call the place "Solitude," and that name will explain almost everything about it. If I hadn't owned that land and been able to escape the cacophony of New York City to be with myself from time to time, my spirit would surely have perished, my soul been mutilated beyond repair. I'm only a hundred thousand or so short of finishing the thing, so if you hear of an angel, let me know. I'd hope to use the first Solitude Retreat to show every town and village, every big city neighborhood, how easy and valuable it is to provide such a public resource — a place where one can be alone with oneself, with no schedule, no agenda, no lectures, no classes, no planned recreation.

And I'm up to some major mischief, trying to produce a long definitive documentary film about the history and the anomalies of (as well as the antidotes for) modern institutional forced schooling. I'm only six or seven million short on that project — but a script is in hand, a national network of assistants created, a production crew organized, and a sample made. If you think of Ken Burns' *Civil War*, you'll get an idea of the scope of the project. Incidentally, the former student who badgered me into writing "Psychopathic School" — and through it, this entire book — is a fine filmmaker; he'll be the director.

Both these undertakings are discussed at some length on my website (www.johntaylorgatto.com), where, if the daemon overtakes you, you can also send me your thoughts from time to time. I can't promise to answer because, like you, I'm often overwhelmed, but I do promise to read every communication twice and to think hard about what you say — and if our paths ever cross, the first Iron City is on me.

God's mercy on us all,

John Taylor Gatto
Oxford, New York
January 2002

Postscript, 2005

From the Publisher

ON APRIL 7, 2004, the *Mid-Hudson Highland Post* carried an article about an appearance that John Gatto made at Highland High School. Headlined "Rendered Speechless," the report was subtitled "Advocate for education reform brings controversy to Highland."

The article relates the events of March 25 evening of that year when the second half of John Gatto's presentation was canceled by the School Superintendent, "following complaints from the Highland Teachers Association that the presentation was too controversial." On the surface, the cancellation was in response to a video presentation that showed some violence. But retired student counselor Paul Jankiewicz begged to differ, pointing out that none of the dozens of students he talked to afterwards were inspired to violence. In his opinion, few people opposing Gatto had seen the video presentation. Rather, "They were taking the lead from the teacher's union who were upset at the whole tone of the presentation." He continued, "Mr. Gatto basically told them that they were not serving kids well and that students needed to be told the truth, be given real-life learning experiences, and be responsible for their own education.

[Gatto] questioned the validity and relevance of standardized tests, the prison atmosphere of school, and the lack of relevant experience given students." He added that Gatto also had an important message for parents: "That you have to take control of your children's education."

Highland High School senior Chris Hart commended the school board for bringing Gatto to speak, and wished that more students had heard his message. Senior Katie Hanley liked the lecture for its "new perspective," adding that "it was important because it started a new exchange and got students to think for themselves." High School junior Qing Guo found Gatto "inspiring." Highland teacher Aliza Driller-Colangelo was also inspired by Gatto, and commended the "risk-takers," saying that, following the talk, her class had an exciting exchange about ideas. Concluded Jankiewicz, the students "were eager to discuss the issues raised. Unfortunately, our school did not allow that dialogue to happen, except for a few teachers who had the courage to engage the students."

What was *not* reported in the newspaper is the fact that the school authorities called the police to intervene and 'restore the peace' which, ironically enough, was never in the slightest jeopardy as the student audience was well-behaved and attentive throughout. A scheduled evening meeting at the school between Gatto and the Parents Association was peremptorily forbidden by school district authorities in a final assault on the principles of free speech and free assembly...

There could be no better way of demonstrating the lasting importance of John Taylor Gatto's work, and of this small book, than this sorry tale. It is a measure of the power of Gatto's ideas, their urgency, and their continuing relevance that school authorities are still trying to shut them out 12 years after their initial publication, afraid even to debate them. — May the crusade continue!

Chris Plant
Gabriola Island, B.C.
February, 2005

Also Available by John Taylor Gatto

The Underground History of American Education
A Schoolteacher's Intimate Investigation into
the Problem of Modern Schooling
(Oxford Village Press, 2000).
448 pages Pb ISBN 0-945-70004-0 US$30.00

A Different Kind of Teacher
Solving the Crisis of American Schooling
(Berkeley Hills Books, 2001)
Pb ISBN 1-893163-21-0 US$23.00

The Exhausted School
Bending the Bars of Traditional Education
(Oxford Village Press/The Odysseus Group, 2002)
120 pages Pb ISBN 0-945700-02-4

— All available from www.johntaylorgatto.com

If you have enjoyed *Dumbing Us Down*, you might also enjoy other

BOOKS TO BUILD A NEW SOCIETY

Our books provide positive solutions for people who want to
make a difference. We specialize in:

Educational and Parenting Resources • Nonviolence
Sustainable Living • Ecological Design and Planning
Natural Building & Appropriate Technology • New Forestry
Environment and Justice • Conscientious Commerce
Progressive Leadership • Resistance and Community

For a full list of NSP's titles, please call **1-800-567-6772** *or check out our web site at:*

www.newsociety.com

NEW SOCIETY PUBLISHERS